INDIGNATION

A Psychological Profile of the Infamous John G. Jones

ANDREWS PRESS
Chicago, Illinois

INDIGNATION

A Psychological Profile of the Infamous John G. Jones

Daryl Lamar Andrews

Indignation:

A Psychological Profile of the Infamous John G. Jones

Published in 2023 by
Andrews Press
Chicago, Illinois 60652

Printed in the United States of America

ISBN: 978-0-9835609-1-3

Table of Contents

Dedication

This work is dedicated to
those who have not taken a full account of
a rising star who fell because of an enormous ego.

It is dedicated to historians who
have often wondered about the mental state of
egotistical men.

It is dedicated to men who
fully espouse true Masonic values
implementing them in their daily lives and
continually working to better themselves.

It is dedicated to male and female
leaders of social and fraternal organizations to
provide considerations for leadership.

It is also dedicated to the
future generations of leaders so that they may
avoid the pitfalls of the past and
learn to find the proper mechanics to
help them stay strong under pressure.

Finally, it is dedicated to my seeds and
to the seeds of all readers so
they understand the negative connotations
associated with poor leadership.

Preface

Many accounts of the Masonic rise and fall of the infamous John G. Jones have been authored. They have provided a clear timeline of his efforts and activities. However, his mindset during these timeframes has always been in question and his activities were not limited to the Masonic ranks but also inclusive of civic actions that were actually beneficial to others. The common factor seems to be his indomitable will for control.

In this work, a psychological profile has been developed from the historical timeline to better understand the thought processes of Jones through his travels in legitimate and illegitimate Masonic circles. The profile has been created via the 1928 DISC Emotional and Behavioral Theory by psychologist William Moulton Marston. An online

DISC evaluator was leveraged to determine the profile type of Jones and other leaders of factions during the late 19th and early 20th Centuries. The profile types provide the psychological review of their personalities and a common basis for comparison against the profile type of John G. Jones.

Interesting tidbits are revealed in the profiles which provide more insight into the method of madness of John G. Jones. His influence was felt across all of the available Masonic Bodies of the era as well as the civic arena in Illinois and beyond. He impacted them in multiple ways but also was a slave to his own ego. Ultimately, his impacts caused more damage to be done than good.

Let the unraveling begin...

1

Chapter One:
COMMITTEE OF ONE

John G. Jones is one of the most infamous characters in the realm of Freemasonry. His exploits appear to have stretched beyond any existing Masonic boundary or perceived boundaries that were in place during his era. Yet, he drove forward anyway with a full knowledge of Masonic law and protocols and did so defiantly.

Were egotistical factors the driving force behind his efforts? Was it an attempt to cover up shortcomings at the heart of his movements? Was he simply corrupted by power or perceived power? Was he a lowly "title chaser" with surreptitious intent? Based on the information gathered, he seems to have embodied all the above. But was he also enabled? This also appears to have been the case.

Ego is an essential characteristic in all human beings. It defines who a person is. It is, in essence, personal reverence intrinsic to every individual. It is low in some cases and extremely high in others. Those with low self-esteem do not hold themselves in high regard. In many instances, they tend to be taken advantage of or tend to become bullies who extort others for their own ends.

Those with high self-esteem typically hold themselves to higher standards and, at times, hold others to standards that are above their standing. No one is without an ego. Whether self-esteem is low or high, an overpowering ego can be of great danger particularly if vanity or pride are her true aims.

Jones appears to fit in the latter category. This is expressly shown through his early rise with the Masonic ranks. A man a high self-esteem, he was most definitely a high achiever with standards that appear to have gone through the roof. He apparently had a well-polished skill set along with charisma to have been elevated and supported within a very short span.

Illustration of John G. Jones

There are two levels to Freemasonry. The Lodge level is the local body of Freemasonry which is segregated within a Masonic Jurisdiction. The Jurisdiction is a region under the control of a parent organization or a Grand Lodge. Within the United States of America, Grand Lodges are typically segregated by states while Lodges are usually segregated by cities within the state or regions within large cities. For example, the City of Chicago is a metropolis which contains multiple Lodges. The Lodges are situated within specific boundaries to avoid overlap. The Grand Lodge of Illinois is the parent organization for all Lodges in the state. As such, the parent and its children comprise a Masonic Jurisdiction.

A Worshipful Master is the elected leader of a local Lodge with Senior and Junior Wardens who serve as the second and third in command of the Lodge. The Grand Master is the Chief Executive Officer of the parent organization. He along with his slate of officers, whose offices are prefixed with the word "Grand", maintain accountability for the entire jurisdiction. Local Lodges report to the Grand Lodge and, in the modern era, one must have served as a Worshipful Master to be eligible for election to a Grand Lodge office. This, unfortunately, was not the case in the early days of the Grand Lodge of Illinois.

Before earning the moniker "Father of Clandestine Masonry", Jones was considered one of the most prominent African American Freemasons alive. He was initiated, passed, and raised in John Jones Lodge #7 in 1871.[1] He was appointed Senior Deacon of the Lodge in 1872.[2] He became an elected Grand Lodge Officer of the Most Worshipful Prince Hall Grand Lodge of Illinois as Grand Secretary while serving as Senior Warden for his Lodge in 1873.[3]

The Office of Grand Secretary represents the Chief Operating Officer of the Grand Lodge. For Jones to have achieved this feat with less than being a year and a half in Freemasonry was extraordinary. He served as Grand Secretary until his election to the Office of Deputy Grand Master of the Grand Lodge in 1875. He was elected

---

[1] Proceedings, Most Worshipful Grand Lodge, FAAYM, IL, 1871, p.28
[2] Proceedings, Most Worshipful Grand Lodge, FAAYM, IL, 1872, p.30
[3] Proceedings, Most Worshipful Grand Lodge, FAAYM, IL, 1873, pp.30,40

Worshipful Master of John Jones Lodge #7 in 1876. He was also appointed District Deputy Grand Master for the Grand Lodge for the entire Northern District while serving as Deputy Grand Master.[4] This only lasted one year as he did not gain election to any Grand Lodge Office in 1876.

Jones was highly active at the 1877 Annual Communication of the Grand Lodge. He was active on multiple committees and even re-introduced a resolution from 1872 for the Grand Lodge to withdraw from the National Grand Lodge. He was even nominated for the Office of Grand Master at that session but lost to Most Worshipful Brother John J. Bird of Cairo, Illinois.[5] Considering the brevity of the timeline, his advancement in Masonic Offices in his first five years within the Order was spectacular.

Bylaws changes were introduced to the Grand Lodge within a few years of Jones' swift elevation to prevent

---

[4] Proceedings, Most Worshipful Grand Lodge, FAAYM, IL, 1875, pp.36,41,46

[5] Proceedings, Most Worshipful Grand Lodge, FAAYM, IL, 1877, pp.34, 39-40

Masons from serving in elective Grand Lodge offices who had not served as Worshipful Master of a Lodge. Updates to Article Two Section Two were presented at the 1875 Grand Communication to this effect.[6] Jones was not the first to achieve this task but was the last. The first was actually Right Worshipful Brother Harrison D. King who was the chairman of the convention to organize a Grand Lodge in Illinois and her first Deputy Grand Master while serving as Senior Warden.[7] However, just as Masonic salutations build upon one another, so should knowledge and leadership experiences. For example:

- **BROTHER** - The most important salutation for any Mason is "Brother" or "servant in arms".

- **WORSHIPFUL BROTHER** - Upon serving the Office of Worshipful Master, the salutation becomes "Worshipful Brother" whose act of worshipping or meditation should produce clear, well-thought-out

---

[6] Proceedings, Most Worshipful Grand Lodge, FAAYM, IL, 1875, pp.46-47
[7] Proceedings, Most Worshipful Grand Lodge, FAAYM, IL, 1867, pp.3-7

plans for the Trestle board. A Mason should have also gained expertise on the management of men.

- **RIGHT WORSHIPFUL BROTHER** - Upon gaining election to Grand Lodge Office, the salutation becomes "Right Worshipful Brother". Although not accountable for the entire organization, this Mason is responsible for key components and should learn the impacts of the key components to the grand plan.

- **MOST WORSHIPFUL BROTHER** - Upon earning election to the Oriental Chair of the Grand East, the salutation shifts from "Right Worshipful Brother" to "Most Worshipful Brother" in recognition of the Office of the Grand Master who is most accountable for the organization.

As these salutations are earned, it is assumed that learnings regarding leadership are absorbed. The leader is the primary servant. If a leader has not made suitable proficiency as the primary servant, it is reasonable that he is not prepared to lead at higher levels. As such, actions to prevent elevation to the macro level of leadership for those who have not proven proficiency at the micro level is reasonable.

Perhaps, had Jones been prevented from experiencing such a swift elevation, he may have learned key lessons that would have prevented the permanent tarnishing of his legacy. Management of a Trestle board for a Lodge of sixty-five (65), which was the size of John Jones Lodge #7 in 1876, may have been the proper forum for him to learn how to properly spread the cement of brotherly love.[8] Yet it is reasonable to assume the Grand Lodge duties prevented his full attention at the local level.

Alternatively, maybe he was enabled by the lack of being checked by the membership. Holding elected and appointed offices in Lodges typically come with expectations. If movement was performed without being checked by the leadership and membership of the Lodge, it could also be reasonable to assume that he drove the ship without regard.

---

[8] Proceedings, Most Worshipful Grand Lodge, FAAYM, IL, 1876, p.40

Appointment to the Office of Senior Deacon with less than a year's worth of Masonic knowledge and election to the Office of Senior Warden with less than two years' worth of Masonic knowledge was, most likely, not enough time for one to learn how he should assist the Worshipful Master in the performance of his duties. Maybe, he was not humbled when fulfilling these roles within the ritualistic expectations. If not humbled at the subordinate Lodge level, it is reasonable to assume that the lack of humility would continue through to higher offices. This hints to the notion of enablement because he was not checked.

While humility or the lack thereof could have been a factor for his demise in later years, acceptance of nominations for positions alludes greatly to a large ego for Jones. Presumably, he believed he could perform all tasks associated with all offices he sought despite being relatively very wet behind the ears. But did he really know "Freemasonry"? Most new Masons in the current era are admonished to wait with patience and not to accept a position for which they are not fully versed. Was this same spirit relative to positional readiness at play in the Lodge or did Jones just possess a superior skillset that satisfied the Lodge's curiosities? Was his swift elevation tied to pre-existing relationships or reputation? It is likely that he was fast-tracked for all the above reasons. As such, he was, most definitely, enabled.

The Honorable Most Worshipful Brother John Jones

Jones' familial relationship to his uncle, Most Worshipful Brother John Jones, Past Grand Master of Ohio Prince Hall Masons, and namesake of John Jones Lodge #7, could have been a factor. The uncle was a charter member of the first Lodge organized in Illinois, namely, North Star Lodge #12 when it was under the Grand Lodge of Ohio. He was a charter member of North Star Lodge #1 when it was renumbered under the Illinois Jurisdiction in 1867. It was he who represented the National Grand Lodge and constituted the Grand Lodge of Illinois in 1867.[9] For his labors, John Jones Lodge was organized under dispensation in Chicago, Illinois and warranted #7 on the rolls of the Grand Lodge of Illinois in 1868.[10] He, subsequently, transferred his membership to his namesake Lodge.

In 1871, the Uncle John became Illinois' first black elected official as Cook County Commissioner. His reputation and capabilities exhibited as a leader of the Convention Movement were renown in all circles. This most prominent Freemason, abolitionist, civic activist and one of

---

[9] Proceedings, Most Worshipful Grand Lodge, FAAYM, IL, 1867, p.4
[10] Proceedings, Most Worshipful Grand Lodge, FAAYM, IL, 1868, pp.30

Chicago's wealthiest citizens was held in high regard in all circles despite race or creed.[11] Thus, John Jones Lodge #7 became the likely Lodge to which his nephew, John G. Jones, would join in 1871.[12,13]

Considering this, did John G. Jones fall victim to expectations tied to the Jones name? After all, his uncle was powerful and famous. So why wouldn't he be able to meet the demands of Masonic office especially with a powerful uncle, his Lodge brother, available for guidance?

Further, the initial appearance of the nephew probably confirmed that the apple didn't fall far away from the family tree. John G. Jones must have exhibited characteristics that affirmed a high-quality skill set and multiple capabilities. Many, likely, attributed that to the influence of his uncle.

---

[11] "John Jones: A Black Chicagoan", Illinois Historical Journal, Vol. 80, 1987, p.188

[12] Travis, Dempsey, An Autobiography of Black Chicago, Agate Publishing, 2013, p.1

[13] Proceedings, Most Worshipful Grand Lodge, FAAYM, IL, 1871, p.28

The nephew certainly caught the attention of Most Worshipful Brother William L. Darrow, Grand Master of Illinois Prince Hall Masons at the 1873 Grand Lodge Session who placed him on the Committee for Nominations for that year. The committee returned the name of Most Worshipful Brother Benjamin F. Rogers, the very first Grand Master of Illinois Prince Hall Masons, to return as Grand Master and Jones as his Grand Secretary.[14] Most Worshipful Brother Rogers, subsequently, saw to Jones' retention as Grand Secretary at the 1874 Grand Lodge Session.[15] As such, the pre-existing relationships aligned with evidence of intellectual competency seemed to serve as drivers for the confidence placed in John G. Jones by many.

The 1875 Session of the Grand Lodge held in Mattoon, Illinois at the hall of Eureka Lodge #13 proved to be more of the same. John G. Jones was again placed on the Committee on Nominations. The committee returned the slate of nominations with Rogers as Grand Master and Jones as Deputy Grand Master or second in command of the

---

[14] Proceedings, Most Worshipful Grand Lodge, FAAYM, IL, 1873, p.30
[15] Proceedings, Most Worshipful Grand Lodge, FAAYM, IL, 1874, p.23

Grand Lodge of Illinois The only office for which the slated nominee did not win election in 1875 was the Office of Grand Lecturer where J.H.C. Hall lost election to Most Worshipful Brother Isaac H. Kelly.[16] However, the slate achieved its purpose in keeping Most Worshipful Brother Rogers at the helm and elevating Jones as his eventual successor.

The attempt to re-elect all officers in 1876 left John G. Jones in the cold. He was slated to retain the Office of Deputy Grand Master but was dealt a slice of humble pie. Maybe his style of leadership was not up to snuff as expected by the Masonic community at large. Maybe the Craft felt the need to halt his swift advancement for other reasons. Despite the loss, Jones retained key appointments to the Committee on Foreign Correspondence and remained an ardent bulldog for the Grand Lodge particularly as it related to her relationship with the National Grand Lodge.

---

[16] Proceedings, Most Worshipful Grand Lodge, FAAYM, IL, 1875, pp.36-37

On June 21, 1872, his uncle John initially submitted the following resolution for the Grand Lodge to withdraw from the National Grand Lodge:[17]

> *Whereas, it has become patent to all well-informed Masons, that there cannot exist legally any Masonic power above a State Grand Lodge;*
>
> *And, Whereas, the so called MWNGL has arrogated itself to the supreme Masonic authority of these United States, and thereby making the State Grand Lodges and Grand Masters subordinate to the said compact;*
>
> *And, Whereas, all Masonic authority, both ancient and modern, have decided and now maintain that a State Grand Lodge, when in session, is supreme in the State and its jurisdiction, and when not in session, the Grand Master assumes supreme power and authority;*

---

[17] Proceedings, Most Worshipful Grand Lodge, FAAYM, IL, 1872, pp.12-13

Now, therefore, be it resolved that the MWGL for the State of Illinois and its jurisdiction now working under the MWNG Lodge of the US&A, after paying all dues to the date of this session, will and do by these resolutions, absolve all relations and connections whatsoever with the above named compact;

Resolved, that this Grand Lodge, and its subordinates, will and do recognize all genuine Masons after due trial, strict examination or lawful information, wheresoever we may find them;

Resolved, that the MWG Lodge for the State of Illinois, do, by these resolutions, instruct the MW Grand Master to be elected at this Grand Communication, to notify the MWNG Secretary by sending him a copy of these resolutions, or cause the same to be done, of the action of this MWG Lodge;

Resolved, that this MWG Lodge do order the warrant and all dues (or money) that may be owed to or claimed by the MWNG Lodge, to be forwarded to that compact, if such a body of Masons can be found, without delay;

Resolved, that this MWG Lodge call a convention to convene on — date and place, for the purpose of organizing an Independent Grand Lodge for the State of Illinois and its jurisdiction.

Discussions on the resolutions were held through the days that followed and, on June 24, 1872, they were referred to a special committee and held over until the 1873 session.[18]

Unfortunately, actions relative to the National Grand Lodge stalled due, in part, to the absence of the uncle at the annual sessions for the years that followed. John G. Jones took up the cause. By 1876, several Grand Lodges had withdrawn from the National Grand Lodge including Illinois' Mother Grand Lodge, the Grand Lodge of Ohio. However, Illinois remained at a stalemate with prominent Masons on both sides of the conflict until it was finally resolved in 1877.

---

[18] Proceedings, Most Worshipful Grand Lodge, FAAYM, IL, 1872, pp.17-18

Right Worshipful Brother Richard E. Moore

The 1877 Session of the Grand Lodge found John G. Jones nominated again for Grand Master by the Committee on Nominations appointed by Most Worshipful Brother Rogers who was a supporter of Jones and along with the Grand Secretary, Richard M. Hancock. The slate found nominations for Jones as Grand Master, James H. Kelly as Deputy Grand Master, J.H. Washington as Senior Grand Warden, G.J. Smith as Junior Grand Warden, J.S.D. Lee as Grand Treasurer, Richard E. Moore as Grand Secretary and Most Worshipful Brother Rogers himself as Grand Lecturer.

However, the slate was challenged by independent candidates for Grand Master, Junior Grand Warden, Grand Treasurer and Grand Secretary. Although Jones' resolution to withdraw from the National Grand Lodge passed, the only slated officer to survive the onslaught was Richard E. Moore, Grand Secretary who defeated Hancock.[19]

The 1878 Grand Communication did not find John G. Jones nominated for elective Grand Lodge office but did find his brother, Theodore Wellington Jones, also of John Jones Lodge #7, independently nominated for Grand Lecturer and duly elected.[20] He was also a neophyte within the Masonic ranks having joined the Lodge in 1875 but he was a man of great means. About four years younger than his brother, he owned a moving and storage company and was held in high regard in fraternal and business circles.[21]

---

[19] Proceedings, Most Worshipful Grand Lodge, FAAYM, IL, 1877, pp.39-40

[20] Proceedings, Most Worshipful Grand Lodge, FAAYM, IL, 1878, p.58

[21] https://recollections.wheaton.edu/2009/07/a-republican-cook-county-commissioner/, retrieved December 2, 2022

Right Worshipful Brother Theodore Wellington Jones

The 1879 Grand Lodge Communication did find John G. Jones slated for the Office of Deputy Grand Master by the Committee on Nominations. He, however, accepted nomination as an independent candidate for the Office of Grand Master but lost to the incumbent, Most Worshipful Brother James W. Taylor. Richard E. Moore also retained election as Grand Secretary for the Grand Lodge.[22] Thus, the 1879 loss ended the aspirations to the Office of Grand Master by John G. Jones but seemed to become the start of

---

[22] Proceedings, Most Worshipful Grand Lodge, FAAYM, IL, 1879, p.24

a long-standing rivalry between him, Taylor and Moore that would have impacts in Appendant Masonic Bodies.

The 1879 loss in particular can be utilized as a prime point of examination of the mental and emotional impact of a swift rise and fall on Jones. Impacts to his ego can certainly be understood. Suffering from wounded pride undoubtedly entered his psyche. They may have been the cause for increased efforts by Jones in other areas of Freemasonry.

Consider that he experienced an extremely swift elevation. The elevation began with support from multiple avenues. To have been an elected Grand Lodge Officer within two years of membership is phenomenal. He seemed to have been held in high regard prior to entering the Masonic ranks and apparently knew how to wield some authority. So, he was on a track for leadership immediately upon obtaining membership.

His swift election was also abnormal. This provides an indication of the amount of support that he had from the start. It seems to have created a sense that leadership for him was predestined locally and at the highest levels. Was he given these expectations before he entered the doors of Freemasonry? Was he, then, brought to the door of Freemasonry for the wrong reasons? It is highly likely that he was been puffed up by supporters and developed delusions of personal grandeur resulting in ultra-egotism.

Although Jones did not appear to purport any ill will or devious intentions when climbing the ranks, vainglory due to a sense of entitlement was apparent. Considering the number of times he sought the Office of Grand Master, he felt entitled. He became a "trophy seeker" which appeared to become his true aim. Although he was skilled and active on multiple committees for the Grand Lodge, attaining the title appeared to become more important than the good of the Order. In conclusion, pride and vanity appeared to rule.

"Pride goeth before destruction, and a haughty spirit before the fall."[23] Entitlement, vanity, pride and egotism led to an early Masonic demise. He certainly must

---

[23] The Holy Bible, KJV, Proverbs 16:18

have felt a strong sense of betrayal from those who originally provided support. The waning support and the fall, however, resulted in wounded pride because he was puffed up and then blown up.

As a Mason with an "Alpha-Male" mentality, it would be reasonable for him to have some resentment after being blown up. While details on sentiments towards his efforts are unavailable, his activities in the remaining quarter of the 19th Century may provide more insight into this. Before exploring that angle, another angle to consider is, had Jones not been blown up, would he have made a good leader of Masons? Applying his characteristics to a theory of motivational needs by Henry Murray, a psychologist, provides some insight into this possibility.

According to Murray, there are four motivational needs that drive top performers to seek leadership positions. Achievement refers to the desire to do things better. Top performers tend to choose more difficult tasks to prove their ability to succeed. Power refers to the desire for influence, domination and prestige. Taking on higher responsibilities by way of positional trophies becomes an opportunity to further dominate. Affiliation refers to the desire to spend time with other people. Social comparisons and attention are factors in this motivation. Lastly, intimacy refers to the desire to build strong relationships particularly as it relates to one-on-one interactions.[24] Measurements according to these factors can help to predict the quality of leadership.

Jones clearly was a high achiever. He took on positions at the local Lodge and Grand Lodge levels immediately. The responsibilities of the Office of Grand Secretary for any Masonic jurisdiction are arduous tasks that require strong administrative and management skills to perform. Based on the meticulous Proceedings and reports provided during his terms of office, his ability to perform the associated tasks were stellar.

His success at Grand Lodge level tasks were also significant escalations from those tasks he performed as

---

[24] Caprara, Gian Vittorio, Daniel Cervone, Personality: Determinants, Dynamics, and Potentials, Cambridge University Press, 2000, pp.348-349

Senior Deacon and Senior Warden in his Lodge. While the former is more of a ritualistic position, the latter is the second in command of a Lodge. It is a critical position which is meant to prepare the officer for the next level of command. Considering that he did all the above simultaneously, his success in these roles confirmed that he was able to multi-task well.

The desire for power in Jones was also obvious. He sought to serve as Deputy Grand Master while serving as Worshipful Master for his Lodge. He had already proven his ability to multi-task and that he had a great understanding of administration at the jurisdictional level. As such, these roles essentially became trophies or opportunities to display prestige.

The higher duties also served as opportunities to showcase skills and dominance. His appointment as District Deputy Grand Master of the Northern region while serving as Deputy Grand Master provided him the opportunity to do this. In the early years of the Grand Lodge, there was a single District Deputy Grand Master who oversaw the entire

District. Jones ran it with an iron fist. His loss in the 1876 election for Grand Master was likely the result of the over exertion of influence.

Jones' desire for affiliation is most certainly in question. Administrative duties in Freemasonry are typically performed in a solitary fashion. In many instances, they do not require much input from others as it relates to the performance of specific tasks. It only takes one person to write an order on the Grand Treasurer. While assistance would be welcomed, it actually only takes one person or less than a handful of people to collect and tabulate receipts. Although he performed his duties well, administrative expertise does not necessarily translate well into the leadership of men.

On committees that Jones participated, was he the dominant force or a considerate leader? Were inputs from others solicited or even considered? Did Jones play well with others? The 1876 election loss is a strong indicator that the Craft did not think so.

As it relates to intimacy, Jones' desire is also in question. One on one relationships were not on equal ground. Partnerships did not appear to be mutually beneficial. The manner of his elevation to Deputy Grand Master in the span of four years could be seen as evidence that the short-term gains from individual relationships were meant for his elevation in the long run. So, they may not have been genuine. Was his service as Grand Secretary an intentional step to gain nomination for the Office of Deputy Grand Master by the sitting Grand Master? Further, was it leveraged for him to be slated for the Office of Grand Master in 1877? Being slated for these positions does indicate the possibility of quid pro quo.

Considering these factors, Jones' profile, at this early stage in Freemasonry, indicates that he was highly skilled, able to multi-task and ambitious but not a great candidate for management. His excellence in achieving specific tasks was on full display as an individual while serving as Grand Secretary. His service as chairmanship of the Constitution and Bylaws, Foreign Correspondence and Condolence Committees in addition to his administrative duties were extensive.[25] The details of each are noted fully in the reports of the 1874 Grand Lodge Communication.

Jones was also lauded by Grand Master Rogers in his inaugural address at the same session. He stated:

> *"May God Bless all, and in particular, our R.W. Bro. J.G. Jones, Grand Secretary, who by his past labors, has merited our future favors – always punctual and no communication from any part of the United States, Canada or Europe, has remained unanswered..."[26]*

Although he was spectacular in these roles, he was ultimately a committee of one. He was a top performer who was used to achieving on his own. Other members were on that specific committee on Foreign Correspondence including John J. Bird and Austin Perry.[27] But were their contributions insufficient for recognition or is this more evidence to a singular approach by Jones? This could be

---

[25] Proceedings, Most Worshipful Grand Lodge, FAAYM, IL, 1874, pp.5
[26] Proceedings, Most Worshipful Grand Lodge, FAAYM, IL, 1874, pp.24
[27] Proceedings, Most Worshipful Grand Lodge, FAAYM, IL, 1875, pp.32

used to reaffirm that Jones' focus on achievement was very high, his focus on power by taking control was also high, his affiliation with other team members was low and intimacy with individuals was, most likely, motivated by a pathway for elevation.

With this in mind, he would not have made a good leader for the Grand Lodge of Illinois. He did not demonstrate superior abilities in the delegation of duties. All indications are that he would have been a micromanager and could have hindered the growth of the Grand Lodge had he been elected.

2

Chapter Two:
FACTIONAL WARS

The late 19th Century seemed to be the era in which John G. Jones weaponized his wounded pride not only within the fraternal ranks but also in societal circles. He also experienced swift elevations in the Scottish Rite and York Rite Bodies and within the legal and political arenas in Illinois. His internal fire for achievement and eternal quest for power was on full display in all areas. As his activity at the Grand Lodge level dwindled after 1879, other avenues presented new opportunities.

The Scottish Rite is an Appendant Rite of Freemasonry that was introduced to African American men in the 19th Century. The leadership structure of the Scottish Rite is very similar to that of a Grand Lodge and local Lodge. However, the regional jurisdictions are different.

The leader of a local Scottish Rite Body or Consistory is the Commander-In-Chief while the leader of the parental body is the Sovereign Grand Commander. The region of the Scottish Rite is national in scope and is styled a Supreme Council versus a state-wide scope for Grand Lodges. Yet, the accountability for the Scottish Rite falls under the leadership of the Sovereign Grand Commander while the local Commanders-In-Chief are accountable for the local Consistories.

Deputies are appointed by the Sovereign Grand Commander to oversee activities in specified sections of the regions. The sections or Orients are segregated, primarily, by state. The Deputies are the official representatives of the

Sovereign Grand Commander in the Orients reporting directly to him on the affairs within the area.

The presence of the Scottish Rite among African American men began after the middle of the 19th Century. Fraters or members of Consistories were sourced from African American Freemasons. As such, the Scottish Rite is considered an Appendant Body of Freemasonry.

By the final quarter of the 19th Century, five (5) Scottish Rite Supreme Councils were active: [28]

1. *Supreme Council for the Northern Jurisdiction (**King David/Darius**) – organized in 1856 under the leadership of Illustrious David Leary – Philadelphia, Pennsylvania;*

2. *Supreme Council for the United States (**USSC**) – organized in 1864 (Compact) by Illustrious Auguste Hugo De Bulow – New York, New York;*

---

[28] Voorhies, Harold Van Buren, Negro Masonry in the United States, Henry Emerson, 1945, pp.60-61

3. Supreme Council for the Southern and Western Jurisdiction (**SC-SWJ**) – organized in 1869 under the leadership of Illustrious Thornton A. Jackson – Washington, District of Columbia;

4. Supreme Council for the Southern Jurisdiction (**Star of Bethlehem**) - organized in 1870 (Compact) under the leadership of Lemuel G. Griffin – Baltimore, Maryland;

5. King Frederick Supreme Council – organized in 1871 under the leadership of Joshua D. Kelley – Philadelphia, Pennsylvania.

There were no clear regional limitations in the nation at the time. So, each Supreme Council sought to extend itself during the Civil War and Reconstruction eras.

Conflicts arose during their expansions. Consistories would be established from African American Masons in the area by Supreme Councils in the same areas. As such, jurisdictional claims were problematic. With the westward expansion of the United States, Illinois became a prime location.

Illustration of Richard Mason Hancock

Prince Hall Consistory was organized in the City of Chicago in 1879 by John G. Jones as a subordinate Consistory of the SC-SWJ with Illustrious Richard M. Hancock was the very first Commander-In-Chief of the Consistory.[29] In 1880, Articles of Incorporation were issued by the Illinois Secretary of State and filed with the Recorder of Cook County by the incorporators including Hancock, William L. Darrow (Past Grand Master) and Jones.[30] In doing

---

[29] Masonic Column, Broad Ax, Chicago, November 25, 1899
[30] Chicago Tribune, August 7, 1880, p.8

so, Prince Hall Consistory secured the City of Chicago, per its standards, for the SC-SWJ.

The USSC challenged the jurisdictional claim of the SC-SWJ through an effort by William L. Dutton to establish a subordinate Consistory in Chicago in 1880. So, Prince Hall Consistory filed suit in the Illinois Circuit Court, Fifth District, claiming that it was the only body that was authorized by the Grand Lodge of Illinois to be the sole provider of the Scottish Rite Degrees and the only legitimate authority in Illinois.[31] After the suit was filed by Edward H. Morris, a temporary injunction was granted by Judge Rogers on August 7, 1880.[32,33] However, the injunction was dissolved days later by Judge Moran who concluded that the matters of a voluntary, fraternal organization would not be decided by the court.[34,35] The matter was subsequently taken up by the Appellate Court in January of 1881 with the same

---

[31] Chicago Daily Tribune, August 8, 1880, p.8

[32] Chicago Daily Law Bulletin, Vol. XXVI No. 211, August 7, 1880

[33] Chicago Daily Telegraph, August 8, 1880, p.8

[34] Chicago Tribune, August 11, 1880, p.8

[35] The Masonic Review and the Masonic Journal, Volume 54, Wrightson & Co, 1881, p.119

result.[36] As the Court did not support anyone's claim, Illinois became a battleground state.

Most Worshipful Brother Dr. Peter W. Ray, M.D.

In 1881, the five Supreme Councils had been negotiating consolidation to present a united front across the nation. On January 13, 1881, they resolved to consolidate into a Northern Jurisdiction and Southern

---

[36] The Inter Ocean, January 10, 1881, p.6

Jurisdiction to cover the nation. At the planned follow up meeting in February of 1881 to perfect the union for the Northern Jurisdiction, the USSC did not attend as Sovereign Grand Commander Dr. Peter W. Ray, felt that the USSC held the only legitimate claim to the Scottish Rite Degrees.[37] The source of his angst appears to be the 1880 suit and 1881 appeal in Chicago which challenged the USSC's legitimacy. Never-the-less, a second meeting occurred on April 9, 1881 between the King David (Darius) and the King Frederick Supreme Councils and they consolidated to form the United Supreme Council, Ancient and Accepted Scottish Rite of Freemasonry for the Northern Jurisdiction (USC-NJ) with William H. Cooper as Sovereign Grand Commander.[38]

Years later, Illustrious Ray revealed his thoughts on the USSC's legitimacy in a letter seeking recognition from the Supreme Council of the Northern Masonic Jurisdiction (Caucasian). He argued that the USSC was established by

---

[37] Hall, Ludwig S., "Doctor Peter Ray: Physician, Past Grand Master and New York Scottish Rite Pioneer", Prince Hall Sentinel, MWPHGL of NY, May-2014, p.27

[38] Voorhies, Harold Van Buren, Negro Masonry in the United States, Henry Emerson, 1945, pp.60-61

Illustrious Auguste Hugo De Bulow, a legitimate authority from the Supreme Council of France.[39] De Bulow, however, established it against France's dictates because he was aware that other Supreme Councils existed in the region.[40] Although the Northern Masonic Jurisdiction concurred with Ray, the USC-NJ pressed forward independently.[41]

The perfection of the union for the United Supreme Council, Ancient and Accepted Scottish Rite of Freemasonry for the Southern Jurisdiction (USC-SJ) occurred six years later.[42] The SC-SWJ and the Star of Bethlehem Supreme Council resolved to merge in 1886 and completed the union in 1887 with Rev. James A. Handy as Sovereign Grand Commander.[43] Prince Hall Consistory was absorbed under its umbrella.[44] Despite the conflicts, the USSC did eventually

---

[39] Letter from Dr. Peter Ray, Sovereign Grand Commander, United States Supreme Council to the Supreme Council, Northern Masonic Jurisdiction, September 1884

[40] Stevens, Albert C., The Cyclopedia of Fraternities, Press of J.J. Little, 1896, p.77

[41] The Masonic Review, Volume 70, C. Moore, 1888, p.139-140

[42] USC SJ PHA, http://aasrphasj.org/usc-history, retrieved 12/2/2022

[43] Evening Star, January 31, 1887, p.4

[44] Voorhies, Harold Van Buren, Negro Masonry in the United States, Henry Emerson, 1945, p.61

establish Excelsior (later Occidental) Consistory in Chicago in 1889.[45] With both Consistories in place, the competition for quality Master Masons was in full effect.

In Prince Hall Consistory, Jones held great influence particularly through his relationships with Commander-In-Chief Hancock, Dillard W. Dempsey and Past Grand Master Darrow. He drove this coalition which sued the USSC to prevent its attempted Chicago invasion. All are listed on the suit as filers.

Hancock was also a well-known Mason and civic activist. Prior to his death in 1899, he was just as popular as Jones.[46] Dempsey was a member of John Jones Lodge #7 and was an ardent Jones supporter. Past Grand Master Darrow was also well known. All excelled in Freemasonry to a degree by way of mutual support.

---

[45] Richardson, Clement, The National Cyclopedia of the Colored Race, Volume 1, National Publishing Company, 1919, p.147

[46] Obituary, The Inter Ocean, June 6, 1899, page 3

Year	Illinois Scottish Rite		
	Prince Hall Consistory	Excelsior Consistory	Occidental Consistory
1879-81	• Richard M. Hancock, *Commander-In-Chief* • John G. Jones, *Grand Secretary*		
1382-88	*Grand Secretary*		
1389-92	• John W. Dunmore, *Commander-In-Chief* • John G. Jones, *Grand Secretary*		
1393-95		• Henry Graham, *Commander-In-Chief* • Richard E. Moore, *Recorder*	
1396	• John G. Jones, *Sovereign Grand Commander Bogus Supreme Council incorporated in 1896)*		• Henry Graham, *Commander-In-Chief* • Richard E. Moore, *Grand Secretary*
1397-98	• Champion. J. Waring, *Commander-In-Chief*		• Benjamin S. Harris, *Commander-In-Chief* • Richard E. Moore, *Grand Secretary*
1899-1903	• Rev. William Gray, *Commander-In-Chief*		• Robert C. Waring, *Commander-In-Chief* • Richard E. Moore, *Grand Secretary*

Chart A – Illinois Scottish Rite

Right Worshipful Brother Hancock served as Grand Secretary of the Grand Lodge from 1868 to 1870 and 1877 to 1878. He also served as Senior Grand Warden in 1872 while Darrow served as Grand Master.[47] He was considered to be capable and qualified in handling administrative roles until challenged at the 1879 Annual Session. He failed to fulfill tasks associated with his office from the 1877 and 1878 Annual Sessions.[48] Most Worshipful Brother James W. Taylor also tied him to a certain element:[49]

> *"We would fall short of our duty were we to fail to call your attention to a certain element whose influence has, and is still being constantly used to work discord and confusion in the Craft... Their acts are so nicely hidden under the cover of the banner of truth and justice that other than a very practical eye would fail to discern or detect the deception.... As to the abuse of confidence and trust, the abuse of the*

---

[47] Grand Officers Elected Prince Hall Grand Lodge of Illinois, MWPHGL of Illinois, 1969, p.97
[48] Proceedings, Most Worshipful Grand Lodge, FAAYM, IL, 1879, p.8
[49] Ibid, p.10-11

banner of justice and truth, the colors under their elements have sailed. Some of the abuses practiced can be illustrated by the following example, at our last session held at Moline, Illinois. It was made public that the minutes would be ready within sixty days to go to press. Three hundred and sixty days have passed an no minutes as of yet. Those minutes have been forcibly detained by Past Grand Secretary R.M. Hancock, notwithstanding, I, by virtue of my office as MWGM have requested him to produce the said minutes and turn them over to the proper party, the present Grand Secretary, but without avail. And the withholding of said minutes have materially hindered us in carrying out, altogether, the orders of the Grand Lodge..."

Right Worshipful Brother Richard E. Moore, Grand Secretary, re-affirmed the Grand Master's claims. He further outlined the impacts of the neglect on his office and the Committee on Foreign Correspondence. Hancock was the chair of this committee which included John G. Jones and James H. Kelley.[50] Moore, then, offered a resolution, which was approved by the Grand Lodge, to condemn Hancock's actions as a direct violation of the sovereign will of the Grand Lodge.[51] At the same session, Jones was slated for the Office of Deputy Grand Master but was nominated as an independent candidate for Grand Master.[52] This move was supported by Darrow, Hancock and others who wanted to see Jones at the helm. However, the exposure of the "element" by Taylor and Moore thwarted the attempt.

Hancock's missing minutes could have been integral to the lawsuit filed by Prince Hall Consistory against the USSC had they been available. There is no record of the "Grand Lodge" granting any Scottish Rite Body authority to grant Scottish Rite Degrees. Most Worshipful Brother Taylor made no mention in his annual address at Annual Communication in 1879 or 1880.[53] Right Worshipful Brother Moore also affirmed at the 1880 session that he received

---

[50] The Inter Ocean, October 12, 1878, p.8
[51] Proceedings, Most Worshipful Grand Lodge, FAAYM, IL, 1879, p.13
[52] Proceedings, Most Worshipful Grand Lodge, FAAYM, IL, 1879, p.19
[53] Proceedings, Most Worshipful Grand Lodge, AFAYM, IL, 1880, p.9-11

the Proceedings from 1868 to 1877 from a third party but not the minutes from Hancock.[54] When produced, they contained nothing relative to the Scottish Rite and could have tanked their case immediately.

To the public, the terms "Grand Lodge" and "Grand Consistory" are not necessarily distinct but, in Masonic circles, there is a very clear distinction. Was it intentional for the suit to use the term "Grand Lodge" to lure the Grand Lodge into the suit? Did they intend to make the Grand Lodge choose which body was legitimate? After all, the USSC was supported by the National Grand Lodge from which the Grand Lodge withdrew just a few years earlier per the resolution of John G. Jones.[55,56]. Was it an attempt to instigate a fight with the National Grand Lodge? After all, it was also struggling because many Grand Lodges withdrew. Was the use of "Grand Lodge" in the complaint a reporting

---

[54] Ibid, p.13

[55] Voorhies, Harold Van Buren, Negro Masonry in the United States, Henry Emerson, 1945, pp.60-61

[56] Proceedings, Most Worshipful Grand Lodge, FAAYM, IL, 1877, pp.34, 39-40

error? Either way, the minutes could have confirmed or denied the Grand Lodge's stance at the time of the suit.

Furthermore, there is also a unique singularity with the Proceedings for 1880. The designation of the Grand Lodge was officially "Free and Accepted Ancient York Masons" (FAAYM) which was commonly associated with the National Grand Lodge (Compact). The Grand Lodge Bylaws were updated to reflect this in 1875.[57] The 1880 Proceedings show the change to "Ancient Free and Accepted York Masons" (AFAYM) as an indicator of separation.[58] The details of the change and re-incorporation were also presumed to be a part of the minutes under Hancock's control. The 1877 withdrawal could have re-affirmed broken amity and been leveraged to prove hostile intent by the National Grand Lodge through the USSC. Thus, the Grand Lodge could have bolstered the Consistory's case.

Notwithstanding, Hancock remained Commander-In-Chief through 1882 when John W. Dunmore succeeded

---

[57] Proceedings, Most Worshipful Grand Lodge, FAAYM, IL, 1875, p.46
[58] Proceedings, Most Worshipful Grand Lodge, AFAYM, IL, 1880, p.65

him. Dunmore would serve for the next thirteen (13) years and Jones continued to serve as Grand Secretary.[59] With allies in place, Jones pursued elevation in the SC-SWJ and his own professional career simultaneously.

Prominent Colored Members of the Chicago BAR
(The Inter Ocean, November 15, 1896, p.30)

---

[59] Illinois Council of Deliberation, http://icodpha.org/history, retrieved 12/2/2022

A notary public since 1880, Jones had also moved forward to focus on a strong legal and political career.[60] He experienced the same types of challenges in these areas as he did in Freemasonry due to his strong personality. He was admitted to Illinois Bar on March 25, 1884 and formed a partnership with Ferdinand L. Barnett and Edward H. Morris, the "Dean of Black Attorneys" and the same who filed the 1880 suit for the Consistory.[61] Through this relationship, Jones was elected Chairman of the Colored Lawyers of the Chicago Bar in 1885.[62] He represented everyone without discrimination and gained a strong reputation from his successes. He eventually earned election to the Illinois General Assembly in 1900.[63]

At his core, Jones was strictly opposed to the practices of segregation and discrimination. Although not necessarily an integrationist, he believed in equality and his

---

[60] Journal of the Senate, Illinois General Assembly, 1881, p.185

[61] Michigan Law Journal, Dennis & Company, 1896, pp.390

[62] The Chicago Legal News: A Journal of Legal Intelligence, Chicago Legal News Company, 1886, p.189

[63] Journal of the House of Representatives, Illinois General Assembly, 1901, p.6

wrath was distributed harshly without regard to the color of a person's skin. In doing so, he earned the moniker "Indignation Jones" because of the voracious manner in which he fought.[64]

Jones arranged "Indignation Meetings". These refer to impromptu conventions of citizens to deal with issues that arose during the day and age. For example:

- Jones was the victim of racial discrimination at a hotel in downstate Illinois in 1884. He collaborated with Illinois politician John W.E. Thomas and others to draw up legislation to prevent discriminatory practices. The effort resulted in the Illinois Civil Rights Act of 1885.[65]

- In 1887, Jones was a public opponent to Dr. Daniel Hale Williams' efforts to create Provident Hospital and train black doctors and nurses. Jones felt that it hinted to black inferiority and felt that special needs were not required for

---

[64] Reed, Christopher Robert, Black Chicago's First Century: 1833-1900, Volume 1, University of Missouri Press, 2005, p.308
[65] Ibid, p.265

blacks. He organized a meeting seeking support, but the citizens showed mass support for Dr. Williams.[66] Hancock, a friend of Jones, supported Provident Hospital and became Vice President of the Provident Hospital and Training Center in 1892.[67] The Grand Lodge of Illinois under Most Worshipful Brother J.W. Moore laid the cornerstone in June of 1896 with assistance from Hancock and others.[68]

- In 1888, Jones led the charge to publicly rebuke and express the dissatisfaction of the African American community with the speedy conviction and hanging of Zephyr Davis, foreman at Greene's Boot Heel Factory, for the murder of an Irish American girl.[69] The coroner's jury criticized the factory for employing Davis, a black

---

[66] Hendricks, Wanda A., Fannie Barrier Williams: Crossing the Borders of Region and Race, University of Illinois Press, 2013, p.64

[67] Chicago Daily Tribune, July 31, 1892, p.33

[68] The Inter Ocean, June 8, 1896, p.12

[69] Dale, Elizabeth, The Rule of Justice: The People of Chicago Versus Zephyr Davis, Ohio State University Press, 2001, p.12

man, to supervise white labor and quickly convicted him. The Deputy Coroner, W.E. Kent, also iterated the same. When Cook County Coroner Henry L. Hertz refused to rebuke Kent, Jones convened a convention, condemned them by resolution and blocked Hertz's candidacy at the 1889 Republic Convention.[70]

- The result of an 1889 session produced a resolution to the United States Congress denouncing the treatment of American citizens in the South. The resolution applied pressure to the William E. Mason, Congressman for the Third Congressional District to implement changes in policy to protect these citizens. This resolution was supported by Masonic friends and foes alike including Dr. Williams and Richard E. Moore.[71]

---

[70] "Hard on Hertz: The Colored Republicans of Cook County sit Down on the Coroner: Monster Mass Meeting", The Appeal, October 20, 1888, p.1
[71] Chicago Tribune, January 10, 1889, p.9

The meetings often drew lines between integrationists and self-help/self-segregationists, but they closed the communications gaps within the community and created a forum for expression resulting in some positive changes. Although Jones was volatile in most cases, he was able to garner support on common grounds. While taking on these challenges, he still managed to matriculate in Freemasonry through chaos.

Most Worshipful Brother Joseph W. Moore

In 1887, Jones and his brother, Theodore had been suspended by Most Worshipful Brother Joseph W. Moore for contumacy and revealing Masonic secrets. During this timeframe, the USSC had also established Excelsior Consistory in Chicago to which Jones regularly went on the attack. He often published circulars and wrote articles designed to destroy its standing.[72] Both brothers were later reinstated after settlement of a civil lawsuit by Jones against the Grand Lodge.[73] Despite the hit, Jones and his supporters still earned elevation in the Scottish Rite USC-SJ.

By 1889 in the USC-SJ, Jones, Hancock, Dempsey, Darrow, Robert C. Waring, and John W. Dunmore were Actives. Jones had also been elevated from Grand Auditor-General to Lieutenant Grand Commander and Deputy for Illinois, Indiana, Kansas, Arkansas, Colorado, and Minnesota; and Prince Hall Consistory had also been renumbered #3 on the rolls of the USC-SJ.[74] In December of 1890, Sovereign Grand Commander Jackson had also appointed Dempsey as Deputy for Illinois, Hancock as

---

[72] Indianapolis Recorder, August 10, 1887, p.8

[73] "Circuit Court – New Suits", Chicago Tribune, October 3, 1887, p.9

[74] De Nichichievich, Cte. F.G. & Richard De Boehme, Universal Masonic Annual for 1889-90, Alexandrie, 1890, p.733 [48] The Inter Ocean, December 28, 1890, p.23

Deputy for Wisconsin, Darrow as Deputy for Minnesota, Waring as Deputy for Michigan, and Dunmore as Deputy for Kansas and Grand Master of Ceremonies.[75] So, the Jones team prospered for a time.

In 1895, Jones lost the election for Sovereign Grand Commander of the USC-SJ to Sovereign Grand Commander Jackson. As such, he withdrew from the session and collaborated with supporters to organize the "bogus" United Supreme Council for the Southern and Western Jurisdiction with the following officers: [76]

- John G. Jones, Sovereign Grand Commander
- Richard T. Greener, Lieutenant Grand Commander
- Dorsey F. Seville, Grand Secretary General

On March 26, 1896, the bogus Supreme Council incorporated Prince Hall Consistory.[77]

---

[75] The Inter Ocean, October 18, 1893, p.5

[76] The Tribune Almanac and Political Register, G. Dearborn & Company, 1895, p.130

[77] "New Incorporations", Chicago Daily Tribune, March 27, 1896, p.10

Illustrious Dunmore, the elected Commander-In-Chief of the Consistory, was expelled from the Bogus Supreme Council for gross un-Masonic conduct in 1897.[78] He along with several others including Illustrious Waring and Illustrious Benjamin S. Harris shifted fealty to Occidental Consistory while those, who remained in Prince Hall Consistory, continued operations in a bogus state.

Most Worshipful Brother James W. Taylor

Despite constant attacks, Excelsior Consistory persisted with Illustrious Henry Graham at its helm as

---

[78] The Washington Bee, August 28, 1897, p.8

Commander-In-Chief, Richard E. Moore as Secretary, Joseph Moore, J.W. Taylor and others as members. In 1893, Excelsior shifted fealty to the Supreme Council for the Northwestern Jurisdiction (SC-NWJ) under Sovereign Grand Commander Milton Fields, which was organized on February 21, 1893, with the support of the USSC.[79]

By 1896, not only had Excelsior Consistory change its name to Occidental Consistory, but also disgruntled members of Prince Hall Consistory joined them. Moore had been elevated to Grand Minister of State which is the third ranking office in the SC-NWJ. Together, they drew Illinoisans into the fold.

The Jones and Moore factions also held steady within Holy Royal Arch or Capitular Masonry and the Knights Templar. Like the Scottish Rite, the bodies are also Appendant Masonic Bodies which pulls its membership from African American Masons. Both are branches of the York Rite and their administrative structures mimic that of

---

[79] The Topeka Plaindealer, August 18, 1905, p.1

the Grand Lodge as jurisdictions are typically aligned by state.

Holy Royal Arch Chapters are local bodies that are led by High Priests. The Chapters within a state comprise the Grand Chapter for that state under the leadership of the Grand High Priest. Templar Commanderies are local bodies that are led by Eminent Commanders. The Commanderies comprise the Grand Commandery for the jurisdiction under the leadership of the Grand Commander.

In contrast to the Scottish Rite, leaders of Grand Chapters and Grand Commanderies are elected at the state-wide level. Deputies, who oversee the Scottish Rite affairs for the region, are appointed by the Sovereign Grand Commander. As such, York Rite leadership within the state is autonomous.

A third York Rite Body, Royal and Select Masters or the Cryptic Rite, completes the York Rite trinity. Its structure is similar to the Capitular and Templar Rites. Local Councils led by Thrice Illustrious Masters report to Grand Councils led by the Grand Thrice Illustrious Master.

	Illinois Grand Lodge & York Rite		
Year	Grand Lodge	Grand Chapter, Holy Royal Arch Masons	Grand Commandery, Knights Templar
1879-80	J.W. Taylor, Gr. Master R.E. Moore, Gr. Secretary T.W. Jones, Gr. Lecturer	J.W. Moore, Grand High Priest R.M. Hancock, Grand King W.L. Darrow, Grand Scribe	R.M. Hancock, Recorder #9 (#1)
1880-81	J.W. Taylor, Gr. Master D.W. Dempsey, D. Gr. Master R.E. Moore, Gr. Secretary	J.W. Dunmore, Grand Chaplain J.W. Dunmore, High Priest #1 J.G. Jones, High Priest #3	
1881-82	D.W. Dempsey, D. Gr. Master R.E. Moore, Gr. Secretary T.W. Jones, Gr. Lecturer	J.W. Moore, Grand High Priest Milton Fields, Grand High Priest, Missouri	
1882-83	R.E. Moore, Gr. Secretary B.S. Harris, Gr. Lecturer		D.W. Dempsey, Commander #9 (#1) J.W. Moore, Commander #15 (#5)
1883-84	J.W. Moore, D. Gr. Master R.E. Moore, Gr. Secretary J.W. Taylor-PGM, Gr. Lecturer	J.W. Moore, Grand High Priest R.E. Moore, High Priest #1	R.C. Waring, Commander #1 D.W. Dempsey, Recorder #1
1884-85		George J. Smith, Grand High Priest	
1885-86	J.W. Moore, MWGM		D.W. Dempsey, Recorder #1
1886-87	R.E. Moore, Gr. Secretary J.W. Dunmore, Gr. Trustee	J.W. Taylor, Grand High Priest R.C. Waring, High Priest #1	
1887-88	R.E. Moore, Gr. Secretary	J.W. Taylor, Grand High Priest	J.G. Jones, Commander #1 D.W. Dempsey, Recorder, #1

Chart B – Illinois York Rite

Year			
1888-89			B.S. Harris, Grand Commander R.E. Moore, Grand Recorder J.G. Jones, Commander, #1 D.W. Dempsey, Recorder, #1 R.E. Moore, Commander, #4
1889-90	R.E. Moore, Gr. Secretary	R.E. Moore, Grand Secretary	
1890-91			B.S. Harris, Grand Commander R.E. Moore, Grand Recorder
1891-92			
1892-93		R.E. Moore, Grand Secretary W.L. Darrow, Grand Lecturer J.W. Dunmore, Grand Captain of the Host	B.S. Harris, Grand Commander R.E. Moore, Grand Recorder R.C. Waring, Grand Instructor J.W. Dunmore, Commander #1
1893-94			
1894-95		W.L. Darrow, Deputy Grand High Priest	H. Graham, Deputy Grand Commander B.S. Harris, Grand Treasurer
1895-96		W.L. Darrow, Grand High Priest	
1896-97			H. Graham, Grand Commander
1897-98			
1898-99			R.E. Moore, Grand Commander
1899-1900		J.W. Dunmore, Grand Lecturer J.W. Moore, Secretary #1	R.E. Moore, Grand Commander R.C. Waring, Recorder #1
1900-01			
1901-02			
1902-03			R.E. Moore, Grand Commander

The Capitular Rite, Knights Templar, and Cryptic Rite were introduced to African American men in the 19th Century. For over a century, they remained the trinity of the York Rite. The Knights of the York Cross of Honor was established in the late 20th Century to recognize York Rite Masons who have led a Capitular Chapter, Templar Commandery and a Cryptic Council. As such, the historical trinity evolved into a quartet of light.

While the focus of the Scottish Rite is philosophy, the collective focus of the York Rite is faith. The Holy Bible is a key source through which more light is revealed. Together, they promote the conversion of faith into practical action for the betterment of the world.

Factional elevation within the leadership ranks of the York Rite was lopsided. Jones supporters hit ceilings while the Moore faction ran the show. Besides Darrow, no other Jones supporter achieved elevation to state-wide leadership through the turn of the 20th Century.

Although the Cryptic Rite, had been established, neither a Grand Council nor local Councils were active in

Illinois among African American men until 1894. The Cryptic Rite Degrees were introduced in Scotland in 1877 when Scottish Royal Arch Masons worked the degrees. The Scottish Grand Council was constituted in 1880.[80] Fourteen years later, after investing Jones and several others with the Degrees, the Scottish Grand Council granted them the authority to organize the General Grand Council of the Cryptic Rite of Royal and Select Masters for the United States and Dominion of Canada. The General Grand Council was perfected in August of 1894 in Kansas City, Missouri with the following officers at the helm:[81]

- Grand Master – John G. Jones of Illinois
- Deputy Grand Master – Peter Harris of Missouri
- Grand Prior – D.R. Stokes of Texas
- Treasurer – R.W. Freeman of Nebraska
- Recording Secretary - Tom W. Logan of Missouri

---

[80] An Overview of the Royal and Select Masters, https://www.gcirsm.org.in/rsm-about-overview.php, retrieved 12/2/2022

[81] The Appeal, September 1, 1894, p.1

- Corresponding Secretary – James F. Rickards of Chatham, Ontario, Canada

Although no subordinate Councils were introduced in the State of Illinois until the 20th Century, Jones retained control over the organization through the early 20th Century.

Prince Hall Council #8, the first Council of Royal and Select Masters in Illinois, would not be organized until 1923 by the Ohio Jurisdiction. The charter Thrice Illustrious Master was the world-famous entertainer, Dr. Andras Babero.[82] The Most Illustrious Prince Hall Grand Council, Royal and Select Masons, Illinois Jurisdiction also would not be organized until 1984.[83]

The factional phenomena were most clearly defined in the Shrine. On June 1, 1893, Jones received Shrine degrees from Noble Ali Rofeldt Pasha, an Arab and Deputy from the Grand Council of Arabia who visited Chicago during the 1893 World's Fair.[84] Over the next few days, he

---

[82] Cornerstone91.com/history, retrieved 12/2/2022
[83] YorkRiteIL.com, retrieved 12/2/2022
[84] Michigan Law Journal, Dennis & Company, 1896, pp.390-391

along with thirteen others organized Palestine Temple. On June 10, 1893, they established the Imperial Grand Council of Prince Hall Shriners, Ancient Arabic Order Nobles Mystic Shrine (AAONMS) with Jones as the Imperial Grand Potentate.[85] Within months, Shrine Temples were setup across the country.

The basis of the Shrine is the Holy Koran which is the Holy book for Muslims all over the world. The structure of the AAONMS mimicked that of the Scottish Rite as its realm of leadership was national in scope. Local bodies or Temples were under the leadership of Potentates. National leadership of the organization was under the leadership of the Imperial Grand Potentate. Like the Sovereign Grand Commander, the Imperial Grand Potentate appointed Deputies to oversee the affairs of the organization in regions or Deserts and report directly to the top on progress. Historically, membership was limited to Master Masons who held membership in the York Rite or Scottish Rite.

---

[85] A.E.A.O.N.M.S., https://aeaonms.org/history/, retrieved 12/2/2022

Inculcated with the Degrees of the Cryptic Rite in 1894 and a new Supreme Council by 1896, Jones worked to setup Consistories, Councils and Temples all over country and beyond. Liberia had become a target as Jones was appointed Minister of Liberia for the United States of America in 1891.[86] He was very familiar with the republic and its political leadership. So, in 1899, he authorized travel as far as the Republic of Liberia for his Deputy, Owen L.W. Smith of Prince Hall Consistory to confer Degrees for all three Rites. Among the recipients were the President of the Republic of Liberia, William D. Coleman; Secretary of State, G.W. Gibson Sr.; Attorney-General, Julius C. Stevens; and several other high-profile Liberian citizens and Americans residing in the Republic.[87]

Confidence in Jones' leadership across the Scottish Rite and Shrine organizations started to crack after 1896. Skepticism was high because he headed bogus and legitimate national bodies simultaneously while challenging

---

[86] The Literary Digest, Vol. 3 No. 14, Funks & Wagnalls, 1891, p.28
[87] The American Tyler-Keystone: Devoted to Freemasonry and Its Concordant Others, Volume 13, J.H. Brownell, 1898, p.596

the legitimacy of others with great indignation. He purposely published false circulars on the topic through many local and national publications by the masterful hands of Dorsey F. Seville. It was common to see negative articles on others while they lauded themselves.

Illustration of Dorsey F. Seville

Seville, a letter carrier by profession and a very talented writer, joined the editorial team of the Washington Bee in February of 1896 to edit and conduct the column titled "Secret Orders".[88] As the editor for the column, he reported the activities of Jones' organizations as if they all were legally constituted and legitimate Masonic bodies. For example, in 1896, the Jones Supreme Council lauded being recognized by a bogus Caucasian Supreme Council, namely, the United Supreme Council of Louisiana.[89] They held no punches from Illustrious Thornton Jackson stating: [90]

> *"ignorance should not be placed at the head of Masonic Bodies. Because men do not agree, threats have been made by the Jackson faction that they would present charges against men who are employed by the government. This is the way 'niggers' talk and the characteristic of some Negroes."*

Even further, it was reported on December 12, 1896 that Jackson was the one who started a bogus body:[91]

---

[88] The Washington Bee, February 15, 1896
[89] The Washington Bee, August 22, 1896, p.8`
[90] The Washington Bee, November 7, 1896, p.4
[91] The Washington Bee, December 12, 1896, p.8

"This morning Sovereign Grand Inspector John Λ. Bell, called again upon The Press and he had official documents from the Supreme Council, announcing the expulsion of Mr. Jackson from the order. The paper is dated at Chicago, November 7, 1895, and states that on account of his defeat for re-election, Jackson with others had withdrawn from the Supreme Council and attempted to start another of their own, and for this they were expelled."

John A. Bell

The USC-NJ was also not immune from the venom. In July of 1896, Seville published his own commentary relative to the formation of the initial five Supreme Councils and consolidation of 1881 which organized the USC-NJ:[92]

> "...after 1850 5 councils sprang up like mushrooms. In 1881 a Council of Deliberation was held in which so called legal and spurious Councils met in Grand Council and the result was that the bogus and legal Councils consolidate and today there are still eight Councils and the Grand cry is bogus."

The lies were unbridled and Grand Lodges were not exempt from attacks. Jones and Seville commented arrogantly on the powers of a Grand Lodge to agitate them stating:[93]

> "...a Grand Lodge of F.A.M., according to the several subdivisions of the Order, is only supreme over the degrees of the Blue Department and nothing more."

Though the accuracy of the commentaries varied, they hit their marks in the court of public opinion. It served as the fuel, in some instances, that kept the Jones organizations

---

[92] The Washington Bee, July 18, 1896, p.8
[93] The Washington Bee, May 2, 1896, p.8

alive in the midst of key challenges from Milton Fields and Isaac Holland.

Noble Milton F. Fields

Fields was an outcast in legitimate Scottish Rite circles. Initially a member of Jones' Shrine Faction, he became disenchanted. So, he setup his own Grand Council using the same format that he used to create the SC-NWJ. He had been an Active member of the USC-NJ when

Missouri was under its domain. After Missouri shifted to the USC-SJ, he was expelled due to misappropriation.[94] This was the source of his creation of the SC-NWJ.

On March 24, 1894, he secured support to establish the Imperial Council for the United States and Canada from the Potentates of Arabic (Chicago), Medinah (St. Louis), Mecca (Topeka), Mohamedan (Leavenworth), Koran (St. Paul) and Palestine (Hamilton, Ontario).[95] Many of these supporters were members of Consistories under his SC-NWJ including the first officers:[96]

- Benjamin S. Harris, Illinois, Imperial Potentate
- J.R. Copley, Missouri, Deputy Imperial Potentate
- A. Williams, Tennessee, Imperial Chief Rabban
- J.A. Wallace, Kansas, Imperial Assistant Rabban
- H.B. Houston, Minn., Imp. High Priest & Prophet
- O.A. Harris, Kansas, Imperial Oriental Guide
- Henry Graham, Illinois, Imperial Treasurer

---

[94] Walkes Jr., Joseph A., History of the USC AASR PHA NJ USA Inc., USC NJ PHA, 1998, pp.40-43
[95] St. Louis Globe-Democrat, March 26, 1894, p.10
[96] Richmond Planet, April 14, 1894, p.4

- Milton Fields, Missouri, Imperial Recorder
- Richard E. Moore, Illinois, Asst. Imperial Recorder
- W.P. Dabney, Virginia, Imp. 2nd Ceremonial Master
- John H. Wilson, Canada, Imp. Captain of the Guard
- George H. Hughes, Canada, Imperial Outer Guard
- Thomas LeBough, Illinois, Imperial Director
- William Harris, Missouri, Imperial Organist

They were incorporated in Chicago, Illinois on August 3, 1894, by B. Harris, Thomas LeBough and Henry Graham.[97]

Jones responded vigorously through multiple media channels. His commentary during his annual address from the 1894 session of his Imperial Council was reported in the Kansas City Times where he denounced the Fields faction as "bogus fakers – Milton Fields, Charles Prentice, Thomas LeBough, R.C. Waring and their following."[98]

Although Fields challenged the Jones Shrine organization, he actually received some press from Seville

---

[97] Chicago Tribune, August 4, 1894, p.6
[98] The Kansas City Times, August 17, 1894, p.5

relative to the Scottish Rite that would appear to be more positive. He posted the following on May 23, 1896:[99]

> *"Deputy Insp. Generals having the power of Supreme Councils in them invested after 1786. The power was put into the hands of nine inspectors in each Nation, who possessed all of the Masonic Prerogatives in their own district. Two Councils were only allowed for the United States with equal powers in their respective jurisdictions. To-day in the United States there are 12. The Colored Brethren having nine out of that number."*

The two Councils noted were the USC-NJ and the Jones Supreme Council. He published the list of officers elected at the 1896 Session of the USC-NJ and the officers of the Jones Supreme Council. There was no mention of the USC-SJ. Then, he quickly pivoted on the subject of the Scottish Rite by posting news that the Supreme Council for the Northeastern Jurisdiction (SC-NEJ) of the United States was constituted on April 18, 1896 in New York under the leadership of Joseph S. Custis. The body incorporated on

---

[99] The Washington Bee, May 23, 1896, p.8

October 16, 1897.[100] The oddity is that he gave a positive nod to Fields, Sovereign Grand Commander of the SC-NWJ, who installed the officers of the SC-NEJ.

In the same article, he posted John G. Jones' leadership of the Royal and Select Masters, the Jones Shrine and its Imperial Council Board of Directors.[101] To the general public, all of these are seen as the legitimate Secret Orders of Freemasonry. While this held true for the USC-NJ, it certainly did not for the Jones Supreme Council. All in all, the intent to sway the public and potential members towards these organizations was clear.

In October of 1896, a new Masonic body was incorporated by Jones, namely, the Sovereign College of Allied Masonic Degrees for North America. The degrees of Ark Mariner, Secret Monitor, Knights of Constantine, Knights of Three Kings, Knights of Christian Mark, Knights of the Holy Sepulchre, and the Holy and Illustrious Cross constituted the college The first officers were:[102]

---

[100] The Buffalo Sunday Morning News, October 17, 1897, p.2
[101] The Washington Bee, May 30, 1896, p.8
[102] The Washington Bee, October 17, 1898, p.8

- C.W. Newton, Illinois, Sovereign Grand Master
- John G. Jones, Illinois, Deputy Grand Master
- Rev. Peter Lucas, Washington, DC, Grand Abbott
- J.T. Fortune, Virginia, Senior Grand Warden
- John M. Adams, Maryland, Junior Grand Warden
- O.R. King, Maryland, Grand Almoner
- Dorsey F. Seville, DC, Grand Registrar General
- G.W. Cooper, Illinois, Grand Master of Finance

In 1897, Jones moved to the leadership role of the new organization and published additional articles on the Scottish Rite denigrating the USC-SJ. He noted in the Enterprise that his Supreme Council was:[103]

> *"regularly organized and opened with high Masonic honors of Scottish Rite Freemasonry. This Council is now presided over by the Illustrious John G. Jones, 33°, of Chicago, who is Most Puissant Sovereign Grand Commander. This is the second regular and legitimate Supreme Council of the Ancient Accepted Scottish Rite of Freemasonry among colored men in*

---

[103] The Enterprise, January 2, 1897, p.1

the United States, and according to the Grand
Constitution of 1776 and 1786, regulating the
Scottish Rite throughout the world, there can only be
two legitimate Supreme Councils among the colored
Masons in the United States."

At the same time, Jones continued to boast on his
Shrine organization, trouncing all other Shrine factions in its
1897 annual Session. The full commentary was displayed in
the pages of The Washington Bee. He placed the number
of Shriners under his control at 1,326 and the number of
Scottish Rite Masons under his Supreme Council at 5,712.
He even commented on the creation of the Daughters of the
Sphynx of North and South America which he constituted
on September 20, 1897 in Chicago. He left a parting shot at
the Fields organization:[104]

"I wish to call the attention of the craft to the little
band of bogus and illegal so-called colored Shriners,
who have their headquarters at St. Louis, Mo. The
men connected with it are known all over the country
as Masonic crooks and money degree peddlers. They

---

[104] The Washington Bee, October 30, 1897, p.8

never had and have not now the Mystic Shrine degree conferred upon them. The St. Louis factory is a place where all sorts of Masonic degrees are manufactured and fixed for order and high-sounding titles are given. Any mason who goes to the St. Louis factory can purchase a title and get any kind of degree he wishes. And whenever you see or hear a Mason say he hails from the St. Louis factory, either in the Shrine or Scottish Rite, it is a notice to all the world, and is of itself insufficient evidence and conclusive proof to every honest, legal and self-respecting Mason to avoid them as you would the most poisonous and contagious disease."

Seville was in full compliance with all of this and other commentary until a drastic turn occurred in 1898. Jones accused Seville of financial misappropriation in his duties as the Imperial Grand Officer of Community Relations. In defense, Seville published the following in The Washington Bee on October 15, 1898:[105]

---

[105] The Washington Bee, October 15, 1898, p.8

"Washington, D.C., October 1, 1898   This is to certify that I, D.F. Seville and my friends have severed our masonic connections with the Ill. John G. Jones, 33°, of Chicago, Ill. And for good reasons, we have gone under the protection of the Compact Masons of North America."

Captain W.D Matthews

In the same article, he notated that Captain W.D. Matthews was elected Grand Master of the Compact Masons. In the subsequent edition of The Washington Bee, he published the details of the entire scheme titled "The Reason Why There Are Three Factions of Colored Masons in the D.C.":[106]

> "As we all know the first split occurred in 1896. Because the Va. Avenue faction brought 33-degree business in the Blue department for settlement, viz: K.T. Chapter and other bodies, before we split in 1896 and upon the advice and under the direction of the Ill. John G. Jones 33°, of Chicago, Ill., we severed our connections with the Va. Avenue faction. The Ill. (John) G. Jones in a letter dated Feb. 23rd '96, stated that, if necessary, he would come to Washington, D.C. and institute a lodge under the A.A.S.R. , and that it would be legal."

More details were presented in the same article outlining that Jones advised him, by letter dated May 30, 1896, to organize a Grand Lodge, Chapter and Commandery. He also noted that Jones advised him to seek out Capt. W.D. Matthews to obtain a charter for a Lodges if he felt uncomfortable with the charter from the A.A.S.R. [107] Seville,

---

[106] The Washington Bee, October 22, 1896, p.8
[107] The Washington Bee, October 22, 1896, p.8

possibly playing the victim in the article, felt that the defection from the USC-SJ was a mistake and recommended a meeting with Sovereign Grand Commander Thornton A. Jackson to reconcile the break. Yet, Jones declined. [108] So Seville acquiesced and sought to merge the Symbolic Degrees under the Scottish Rite for full Masonic control.

While the full truth of Seville's account is questionable, the full scheme of Jones relative to his break from the USC-SJ in 1895 was revealed. Jones either contrived to move to this pattern before the schism or he pivoted quickly afterwards to this new plan. Either way would not have been done in a truly legitimate Masonic fashion which provides an indication of their true motives.

Seville's editorials were met head on by Jones who escalated the matter to a higher level. Seville was a valued postal employee and Jones attacked him publicly to which the Postal Chief in his office raised concern. So, he published a full financial accounting of his dealings on November 12,

---

[108] Ibid, p.8

1898 covering the years 1895 to 1898 and raised concerns over the financial transactions of Jones noting :[109]

> "These are all the moneys that I have handled, as Mr. Jones is grand commander, grand secretary-general, grand treasurer-general, grand potentate, treasurer, recorder, issuing all charters, patents and rituals direct from Chicago. In his annual addresses made the several grand bodies so fat to date I have first to see any mention of moneys that he has received from time to time."

Jones expelled Seville on December 10, 1898.[110] This prompted Seville to deliver a fatal nail in the coffin of Jones after he again attacked Seville's livelihood by sending a letter of attack to the City Postal Department. He posted in the March 4, 1899 edition of The Washington Bee the full details of the schism in the Scottish Rite from 1895 in an article titled "John G. Jones Again":[111]

> "Mr. Jones forgets that when he came to this city in October 1895, and instituted his so-called Supreme

---

[109] The Washington Bee, November 12, 1898, p.8
[110] Walkes Jr., Joseph A., History of the Shrine, AEAONMS, 1993, p.28
[111] The Washington Bee, March 4, 1899, p.4

Council of Scottish Rite Masonry, which he claimed to be the legitimate united Supreme Council of the Ancient and Accepted Scottish Rite, when it is well known that Mr. Thornton A. Jackson is the legitimate Sovereign Grand Commander. In the near future full particulars will be laid before the masonic world exposing the whole business. Mr. Seville will explain how the 33 degree was conferred in his house October 22, 1895, between the hours 8:30 and 12 o'clock. The whole business will be thrown on the canvass."

The public diatribe between them caused great stirrings in all of the bodies under Jones' control which drove Nobles to take matters into their own hands.

A Shrine faction was created by James H. Hill, Imperial Potentate. Seville had also created the National Imperial Council for North America.[112] Both were based in Washington, D.C. Yet, their organizations would be dwarfed by the faction created by Isaac L.W. Holland.

---

[112] The Washington Bee, June 22, 1901, p.8

Holland, Potentate of Pyramid Temple and Edward A. Turpin, were also suspended by Jones on December 10, 1898.[113] As such, Holland issued a national call to Shrine Temples to discuss reorganizing the Imperial Grand Council based on a patent received from France. The Wilkes Barre Weekly reported:[114]

> *"The weighty document which he carries is a special patent of power secured directly from France, and the object of the call a protest against the continuance in authority of John G. Jones, Chicago."*

The call was answered on December 12, 1900, by Pyramid and Sahara Temples of Pennsylvania; and Magnus Temple of Virginia. They resolved to organize a new Imperial Council proclaiming the following ten points to the world:[115]

1. *"We want to go into a pure convention to set apart and establish a new Temple."*

---

[113] Walkes Jr., Joseph A., History of the Shrine, AEAONMS, 1993, p.28
[114] The Wilkes Barre Weekly Times, December 12, 1900, p.5
[115] The Washington Bee, June 22, 1901, p.8

2. *"We do not want to be under a suspended Mason as our leader."*

3. *"We want every Mason to be under a regular, legitimate grand lodge."*

4. *"We do not want any spurious Mason among this new Imperial Council."*

5. *"We want to adopt a new constitution that we are not ashamed of."*

6. *"We do not want any monarch over our imperial council."*

7. *"We want every noble that is a representative to have a full say in behalf of his temple at any annual session."*

8. *"We want every temple to know what has become of the moneys that are paid into the imperial council."*

9. *"We want every temple to send a representative to the sitting of the new convention for the election of a supreme imperial potentate and imperial officers to govern this body."*

10. *"We propose that each state and territory shall be laid out in four districts and district deputy potentates be appointed and shall have exclusive jurisdiction over his*

district. We want to establish a supreme imperial temple on the basis that every temple will know where their money goes to and for them to have a say where it is to go."

These ten points were a clear response to both Jones and Seville. They were designed to prevent infiltration by the Compact Grand Lodge or any other bodies of Masons from irregular or unrecognized jurisdictions. The new Imperial Council was named the Ancient Egyptian Arabic Order Nobles of the Mystic Shrine (AEAONMS).[116]

With its creation, three (3) primary Shrine factions were in play. Jones still drove his faction with sizeable support and authority over a Scottish Rite and Cryptic Rite domain but the final die had already been cast. It seemed that everywhere Jones went, trouble soon followed which not only drove him to lose members from his Shrine faction year by year but also from other bodies like the Cryptic Rite.

---

[116] Aeaonms.org/history, retrieved December 2, 2022

Year	Illinois Shrine		
	Jones Shrine (AAONMS)	Fields Shrine (AAONMS)	AEAONMS
1393		• Benjamin S. Harris, *Imperial Potentate*	
1394-1895	• John G. Jones, *Imperial Grand Potentate* • Dillard W. Dempsey, *Imperial Chief Rabban* • John W. Dunmore, *Imperial High Priest & Prophet*	• Henry Graham, *Imperial Treasurer* • Milton F. Fields, *Imperial Recorder (MO)* • Richard E. Moore, *Assistant Imperial Recorder*	
1396		• Benjamin S. Harris, *Imperial Potentate* • Richard E. Moore, *Imperial Recorder*	
1397-1898	• John G. Jones, *Imperial Grand Potentate* • Isaac L.W. Holland, *Imperial First Ceremonial Master*	• Joseph W. Moore, *Potentate, Arabic Temple (Chicago)* • Richard E. Moore, *Recorder, Arabic Temple (Chicago)*	
1899-1900	• John G. Jones, *Imperial Grand Potentate*		
1901-1903	• John G. Jones, *Imperial Grand Potentate*		• Isaac L.W. Holland, *Imperial Potentate*

Chart C – The Shrine

Mass defections began to occur at the same time the AEAONMS organization was formed. Alabama Cryptic Masons questioned Jones' intent as early as 1898. James A. Farrier posted in The Montgomery Advisor:[117]

> *"This man Jones, now here in Alabama seeking to inveigle colored men into an organization the rights to organize which has been delegated to me. His whole conduct, including his so-called letter of authority to me, the granting of which he has been base to deny, I regard as fraudulent and believe he is simply here on a scheme to make money out of colored men who are ill able to be paying it to a Chicago sharper."*

He further denounced the National Grand Lodge (Compact) under Captain Matthews, the National Grand Master for irregularities and support of and affiliation with Jones. In 1899, Farrier was expelled from the National Grand Lodge.[118]

---

[117] The Montgomery Advisor, August 9, 1898, p.5
[118] The Birmingham News, October 26, 1899, p.6

These sentiments were not local to Alabama but became a common theme throughout Jones' domain. It had matriculated to the Desert of Iowa and throughout the entire Jones faction. So, on August 5, 1901, Jones cleaned house in Iowa revoking the privileges of all Deputies except for a single loyalist, Isaac L. Brown.[119] At the time, Brown was the Grand Master of the Most Worshipful United Grand Lodge of Masons of Iowa and Its Jurisdiction.[120]

Illustration of Magnus L. Robinson

---

[119] The Bystander, January 24, 1902, p.1
[120] The Bystander, July 10, 1903

The rash actions of Jones and continuous questions on the finances of the Shrine by the officers of the organization were prime factors for the exodus. As time went on, more Shriners began to shift to the Holland faction which, according to its founding principles, was a more open organization compared to the dictatorial stylings of Jones including Magnus L. Robinson.

Robinson served as Imperial Recorder under Jones from 1899 to 1900. It was during his term as Imperial Recorder that a resolution was submitted denouncing National Compact Masons. At the session in 1899, charges were filed against Robinson in 1899 for un-Masonic conduct but were held over until 1900. At the session in 1900, he was found guilty by the Imperial Council of un-Masonic conduct. After being expelled and replaced by John A. Bell, he aligned with Holland and became one of the AEAONMS incorporators in 1901.[121,122]

---

[121] Evening Star, November 19, 1901, p.3
[122] Proceedings, AAONMS, 1901,pp.34-35

By 1901, several detractors including Robinson were also reported to have been expelled by Jones from his Scottish Rite and Cryptic Rite Bodies. Holland and Turpin had already been expelled by Jones by 1899. By 1900, E.A. Williams joined their ranks. At the 1901 session W.H. Moss, Isaac Carper, Frederick S. Monroe, C.A. Knox, Robert Brady, Howard Hill, Walter Billows, Thomas Monroe, R.B. Robinson, H.A. Carter, Isaac H. Layton, B.F. Warner, W.S. Hill and Willier Wright were also expelled.[123] Of them, the following had become elected charter Officers of the AEAONMS under Thomas Holland's leadership:[124]

- C.A. Knox, Imperial Assistant Rabban
- H.A. Carter, Imperial High Priest & Prophet
- Magnus Robinson, Imperial Recorder
- E.A. Turpin, Imperial Assistant Recorder

By the time of Jones' death, the AEAONMS reigned.

Fields also maintained his faction for a decade after the AEAONMS was organized but it had also begun to

---

[123] Ibid, p.35
[124] The Topeka State Journal, September 27, 1901, p.5

crumble. Tired of the conflicts between factions, Temples began to shift fealty to the AEAONMS. Fields, eventually, acquiesced. He shifted fealty to the AEAONMS in 1911 at the Imperial Session held in Atlantic City, New Jersey. Upon doing so, he was acknowledged as an AEAONMS Past Imperial Potentate at the session.[125]

Yet, for Jones to have built so much and then lose it, was tragic at its best. He spent a great deal of time, energy, effort and resources to establish and expand several Masonic organizations at the same time. While some were done in a legitimate fashion, others were spurious in nature. But the split in the Shrine was not the final blow to the Masonic career of Jones in legitimate circles. The final blow was dealt in 1903 in the Blue Lodge.

---

[125] Walkes Jr., Joseph A., History of the Shrine, AEAONMS, 1993, pp.66-67

3

Chapter Three:
ASSAULT ON MASONRY

In 1903, the Grand Lodge of Massachusetts filed charges against Jones for "affiliating and working with suspended, irregular, and clandestine Masons in the City of Boston." While Jones had also filed charges against the Grand Lodge of Massachusetts, they were without foundation and were dismissed by the Grand Lodge of Illinois. However, based on the findings of the Commission and the unanimous vote of the Grand Lodge, Most

Worshipful Brother Henry E. Burris, Grand Master of Illinois Prince Hall Masons, suspended Jones indefinitely. [126]

As a suspended Mason, he still found avenues of leadership. On July 10, 1904, the General Grand Encampment of Knights Templar for North and South America was organized by representatives from Illinois, Ohio, Michigan, Arkansas, California, Colorado and Washington, D.C. The very first elected officers were:[127]

- John G. Jones, Most Eminent Grand Master
- B.J. Fleether, Deputy Grand Master
- Alex Payne, Grand Generalissimo
- J.H. Blunt, Grand Captain General
- S.R. Johnson, Grand Treasurer
- R.E. Jones, Grand Recorder
- H.T. Broudus, General Senior Warden
- W.R. Morris, General Junior Warden
- Thomas J. Riley, Grand Sword Bearer

---

[126] Proceedings, Most Worshipful Prince Hall Grand Lodge IL, 1925, pp.180-182
[127] The Appeal, July 16, 1904, p.4

This provides greater evidence to his remarkable ability to pivot during tragic times. It begs the question. Why was it allowed? There are a few possibilities.

The penal actions of the Grand Lodge against Jones may not have been officially communicated in all circles at the time. The Grand Lodge did not make a habit of publishing internal Masonic dealings in newspapers but did send notifications through the Foreign Correspondence Committee. So, timing could have been an issue.

It is also a possibility that Jones may have convinced the representatives that the charges were unfounded and requested a brief asylum to deal with them. To operate smoothly like no issues were in place seems to be a method that he would take advantage of. Considering also that he ran multiple bodies at the highest levels, it could also have been dealt as a quid pro quo scenario.

Nevertheless, he attended the annual session of the Grand Commandery of Knights Templar of the State of Illinois and its Jurisdiction on August 26, 1904. He installed Right Eminent Grand Commander Frank B. Cranshaw who was also the charter Worshipful Master of Oriental Lodge U.D. (#68), and the other Grand Commandery officers.[128,129] He basically operated like there was no issue at all.

Most Worshipful Brother Henry E. Burris

His victory was short-lived. In October of 1904, Most Worshipful Brother Burris expelled him with the unanimous consent of the Grand Lodge. Jones refused to attend the session.[130] But, it was this final blow that ended thirty-three (33) years of travels for Jones in legitimate Masonic circles.

---

[128] 150th Anniversary Yearbook, MWPHGL of Illinois, 2017, p.112
[129] The Broad Ax, September 3, 1904, p.1
[130] Proceedings, Most Worshipful Prince Hall Grand Lodge IL, 1925, pp.180-182

From a psychological perspective, Jones had to be significantly impacted. His ultra-ego and charisma were strong enough to allow him to start large ventures in the Masonic ranks and navigate through troubled waters. His capabilities in organizing men were undeniably extraordinary. The vanity of being the "first achiever" in the cases of the Shrine, Cryptic Rite and General Grand Commandery of Knights Templar, can certainly be viewed as attempts to claim the trophy of "founding-father". Yet, the ventures that he started tended to be taken over by someone else because humility never appeared to be an important factor in his movements.

The lack of humility is illustrated in fraternal and legal circles. He responded to the loss in the USC-SJ election of 1895 by going on the offensive. Rather than accept the slice of humble pie, heal up and try again, he took an immoral, bogus path. This was also displayed in court and within civic organizations. The Honorable James B. Bradwell, Illinois lawyer, judge and politician, captured the character of Jones best when he stated in relation to Jones "woe unto the man that steps on his toes, and thinks because he is a colored man, he will not resent it. He is ever ready to defend his rights."[131] This radiates a strong sense of personal insecurity to which narcissism and attacks were defensive mechanisms.

When transferring Jones' insecurity and narcissism to the "Motivational Needs Model" of Henry Murray covering the period just prior to his final expulsion, the motivational needs remained consistent. Relative to the achievement and power motivational needs, Jones continued to seek and capture leadership roles. At least one leadership role, "Imperial Grand Potentate" was self-created. So, achievement appears to have been a core motivation for him.

Jones did not necessarily seek to improve an aspect of Freemasonry but appeared to create levels of influence over the people in the Orders he controlled. Interactions with Dorsey Seville can attest to this. Although he did seek to improve the state of the black community through his

---

[131] Michigan Law Journal, Dennis & Company, 1896, pp.390

Indignation Meetings, those on the opposite side of him bore the brunt of a massive assault or show of power over them. So, the improvement aspect became lost in narcissism.

Relative to the affiliation motivational need, connections appeared to be utilized as an avenue to express power and not necessarily for a need to belong. Rather than actively listen to opposing views, Jones contested them immediately. At times, opposing views provide nuggets that can be beneficial in the long-run. For example, the intent of Provident Hospital was not an acceptance of inferiority. It was to provide an under-served community with a lasting option for training. Had it been shutdown, a generation of medical professionals would have been lost. Jones had a severe case of tunnel-vision in this instance and in other situations which led to a continual pattern of being fired.

Jones was fired multiple times. He was fired when the Grand Lodge did not elect him Grand Master on multiple tries in the 1870s. It was clearly a great blow to have been fired from the leadership within the USC-SJ in the 1895 election. It drove him to attack and create a bogus Scottish Rite body. It must have been a great blow for him to have been fired from the Shrine, the one Order that he created himself.

The Honorable Richard Howell Gleaves

Specifically in the Shrine, he was often accused of inequitable treatment. Noble Richard Howell Gleaves certainly would agree with this sentiment as Jones overrode his authority as the Deputy for the Desert of Pennsylvania relative to the creation of Temples and other acts. Gleaves resigned as Deputy due to unfair treatment by the Imperial Council.[132] Holland was expelled for disagreeing with him. As such, it is no surprise that the starting point for the reorganization of the Order emanated from Pennsylvania herself at the hands of Noble Holland.

Milton Fields' defection from Jones' Shrine was most likely tied to conflicts between two bulls. They both had similar track records of dishonor in the Scottish Rite but power struggles often placed them in juxtaposition. These actions confirm that the intimacy motivational need was not wholly in-tact. Initial supporters quickly became opponents and, as Bradwell stated regarding Jones, "woe to the man who steps on his toes."[133]

In leadership, individuals who are extremists and high performers tend to micro-manage and, often, find themselves performing the bulk of the tasks. This explains why Jones, himself, travelled across the country to such a high degree. It would be hard to find any Prince Hall Mason

---

[132] Walkes Jr., Joseph A., History of the Shrine, AEAONMS, 1993, p. 51
[133] Michigan Law Journal, Dennis & Company, 1896, pp.390

in history who travelled as much as he did. He clearly had a lot of plates on his table. Considering the defections and controversies, he was hard-pressed in managing them all successfully. This is another factor that illustrates a lack of intimacy with membership.

There seemed to be a lack of trust overall. It begs the question, was he truly able to develop interpersonal relationships and leverage them for future progress? In the short-term, he had to have been a great spokesman to gain initial support for initiatives. His connection with Dorsey F. Seville is a product of this. He was successful for producing a great gift. Yet, in the long-term, he failed to produce long-term success because he couldn't maintain good and healthy relationships. This is why he kept getting fired. All in all, good leaders have good interpersonal skills which requires a sense of intimacy. After all, there is no letter "I" in the word "TEAM".

Clearly, Jones suffered from a wounded pride. Yet, he was able weaponize it and utilize it to remain relevant. His personality may, initially, have emanated the scent of a strong servant leader but his subsequent actions gave off the vibes of a dictator. The Book of Luke in the Holy Bible provides more insight which reads "he who exalts himself will be humbled, and he who humbles himself will be exalted."[134] Jones was certainly humbled. Yet, rather than heed the second half of Luke's words, he quickly sought to exalt himself again. In doing so, he earned the moniker of the "Father of Bogus Masonry".

Expelled and exposed, shaken, but not stirred, the meteoric rise and fall of John G. Jones was filled with twists and turns like a "James Bond" novel. Within four years of being raised a Master Mason, he was a Past Grand Secretary and the Deputy Grand Master for Illinois Prince Hall Masons. He was slapped down when attempting to obtain the Office of Grand Master. So, he pivoted. Within four years of establishing a Consistory in the State of Illinois in 1879, he was elevated to the Active Grade of a Supreme Council. He was slapped down when attempting to obtain the Office of Sovereign Grand Commander. He pivoted

---

[134] Holy Bible, RSV, Luke 18:14

again. He extended the Cryptic Rite and the Shrine. Due to disgruntled members, the Shrine organization that he created was reorganized while he was still at the helm. After being dealt the final blows by the Grand Lodge of Illinois, history again repeated itself. Jones pivoted.

Many are of the opinion that Jones was expelled due to cause and effect. He conferred Masonic Degrees unlawfully and issued circulars of a split in the Grand Lodge of Illinois. So, the logical result was to suspend him and his cohort, William Gray, indefinitely and later expel them both. It is not a common belief that he intended for all of this to happen to create a new era of Freemasonry.

Consider that Jones had been invested with every single Masonic Degree that was available during the era and even created one himself, the Shrine. A master organizer who had broken or been fired from leadership in most of the Masonic organizations, why bend to the will of others whom he felt were inferior to him? In the Masonic Order and in social and civic circles, he had already proven that he had a superiority complex. So, why even trifle with men who he felt were beneath him? He was alpha-narcissistic incarnate which leads one to believe that he felt the need to beat his opponents with their own tools – Freemasonry.

It could be said that every move made was calculated, that Jones intended to subversively create a new organization under the noses of Illinoisans and others across the nation. He had been knocked out of line for Grand Master, overlooked in the Knights Templar and Holy Royal Arch state-wide leadership offices, and had been smacked down in the Scottish Rite. One could only imagine the thoughts in his mind - "vile miscreants and infamous wretches! How could they do this to me!?! I'll show them. I'll show them all!!!"

John G. Jones, and William Gray were charged, tried, and suspended indefinitely from all the rights, benefits and privileges of Freemasonry for gross un-Masonic conduct on October 14, 1903.[135] On October 22, 1903, the Most Worshipful St. John's Grand Lodge, Ancient Free &

---

[135] Proceedings, Most Worshipful Prince Hall Grand Lodge IL, 1925, pp.180-182

Accepted Masons, of Chicago, Illinois was incorporated by Jones (Grand Secretary), Gray and William H. Davis.[136]

The Honorable Reverend William Gray

This appears to have been a planned disruption and one that was planned well. The conferral of Degrees did occur prior to the session. The team was also already aligned to move forward with the formation of a new body.

---

[136] Chicago Tribune, October 23, 1903, p.13

Had Jones not been expelled, it is highly likely that the "split" would have occurred anyway.

The St. John's Grand Lodge was setup in a position of strength though. As the Grand Secretary, Jones handled all legal and administrative responsibilities. As Grand Master, Gray, the sitting Commander-In-Chief of Prince Hall Consistory under Jones' Supreme Council, kept the locals aligned and made for a clear scapegoat, in the eyes on the law and public at least, if the rouse fell short. He pivoted hard, struck fast, and achieved his goal.

Although the Prince Hall Masonic community was aware of the actions of the Grand Lodge of Illinois, Jones continued to build despite the immense amount of pressure that was against him. He identified areas in the City of Chicago where the presence of Prince Hall Masons was not at a high level. As blacks moved to the southern and west sides of the city, Jones peddled Masonic degrees from the first through the thirty-second within the locales. Many who became residents of the Chicago area due to the Great Migration became duped into what they thought were legitimate Masonic organizations. The Grand Lodge of Illinois established commissions to combat the threat.

Most Worshipful Brother Burris empowered a commission to effectively communicate with suspected members of Jones' groups and absorb them into legitimate Masonic circles. The commission included Richard E. Moore, Joseph W. Moore and others who had a wealth of knowledge on the modes of operation of Jones. Eureka Lodge #64 and Universal Lodge #65 of Chicago, Illinois were immediate products of their efforts.[137] Both were organized under dispensation in 1903 and warranted at the Annual Communication of the Grand Lodge of Illinois in 1904.[138]

Jones fought back by filing suit against the Grand Lodge and specific officers including the Moore Brothers, L.W. Dickerson, R.G. Hall, Frank W. King, and Charles A.C. Smith in the Superior Court of Cook County claiming criminal libel and defamation of character. In the suit, he

---

[137] Walkes Jr. Joseph A., History of the Shrine, AEAONMS, 1993, pp.44-46

[138] Proceedings, Most Worshipful Prince Hall Grand Lodge IL, 1925, pp.180-182

claimed that the grounds for his suspension were based on lies and baseless allegations relative to the issuance of circulars, by him and William Gray, claiming a split in the Grand Lodge and their conferral of degrees without authority.[139] Additional charges were filed against Adam Horn for bearing false witness.[140] All were arrested multiple times and hauled to court to address the suits. Although Horn's charges of libel were found in Jones' favor, nothing significant came from the filings to reverse the decision of the Grand Lodge in the 1903 internal Masonic trial.[141]

Most Worshipful Brother Burris continued to push forward on a higher agenda item while enduring the scourge of Jones. It was under his watch that the Prince Hall Masonic Home was established in Rock Island, Illinois. The initial purpose of the home was to house widows and orphans of deceased members of the Order. This was accomplished in October of 1904 and with Robert J.B.

---

[139] The Broad Ax, February 20, 1904, p.1
[140] The Broad Ax, February 6, 1904, p.1
[141] The Broad Ax, February 27, 1904, p.1

Ellington as the President of the Board of Trustees overseeing the property.[142]

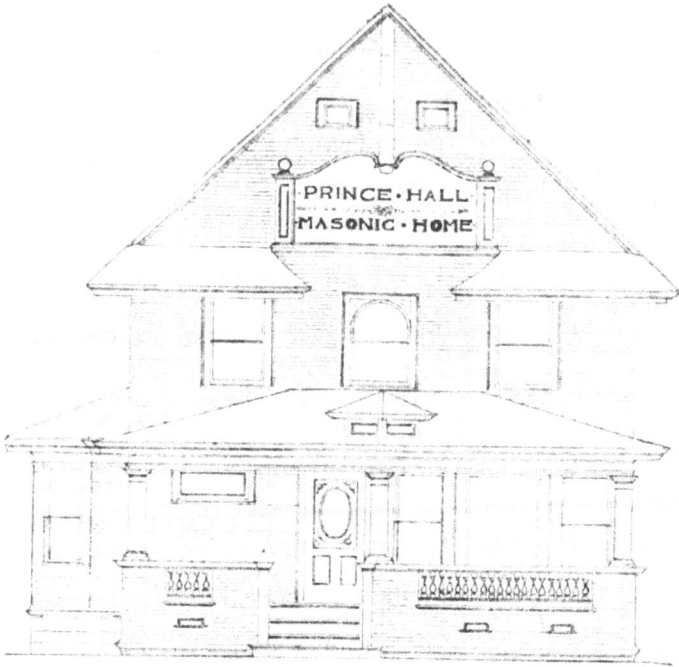

Illustration of the Prince Hall Masonic Home

Efforts for the home continued under Most Worshipful Brother George H. Jesse, successor to Burris.[143] During his tenure, the home became a mainstay for sessions of the

---

[142] The Dispatch (Moline), October 21, 1904, p.2
[143] Proceedings, Most Worshipful Prince Hall Grand Lodge IL, 1925, pp.187-192

Prince Hall Grand Commandery of Knights Templar. Their session held in 1909 culminated in a large picnic hosting Templars from Illinois and Iowa after their 26th Annual Session.[144]

Most Worshipful Brother Jesse continued the practice of sniffing out bogus Masons and working to absorb them into the Grand Lodge of Illinois. Under his watch, Celestial Lodge was secured from the grasp of Jones and warranted in Chicago's Englewood community. The Lodge was chartered on October 8, 1909, and, numbered as #80 on the rolls of the Grand Lodge of Illinois.[145] Jones, who had elevated himself to Grand Master of the St. John's Grand Lodge, attacked Most Worshipful Brother Jesse in the same manner, continued to establish Lodges and continued law suits against Richard E. Moore, Grand Secretary for the Grand Lodge of Illinois and others. Although the courts would not intervene, the "boots on the ground" approach by the Grand Lodge of Illinois was

---

[144] The Rock Island Argus, August 6, 1909, p.12
[145] Proceedings, Most Worshipful Prince Hall Grand Lodge IL, 1925, pp.190-191

partially successful as it steered several good men towards the circle of legitimacy. Yet, despite its best efforts, the St. John's Grand Lodge was able to endure.

In business, men are praised for such achievements. They are praised for success in hostile territory even if the hostility sourced from their own initiatives. After all, it had to take a great deal of guts to move forward and a great deal of savvy to convince others to follow suit. The fact, though, that trial runs had already been done removed the high degree of angst for Jones. Consider, that he created a bogus Supreme Council and flogged the legitimate one while doing so. Fields created a separate Shrine organization in the shadow of the existing one and Holland simply reorganized the Jones' Shrine. These acts set the pattern that Jones utilized to create a subversive empire whose effects still last well over a century after his death.

A point for consideration is that Jones did drive for changes that were beneficial for African American community at large. His efforts in 1884 helped to drive the antidiscrimination legislation that was implemented by

John W.E. Thomas, the Illinois Civil Rights Act of 1885. Although his community meetings were tagged "Indignation Meetings", they did bring issues that impacted African American communities to a large degree.

Jones did drive state-wide meetings and initiate the creation of colored leagues in 1895.[146] Several including the Civic Rights and Justice League and the Afro-American Equal Rights League were prominent. To the public, he was seen as "the colored Chicago lawyer who started the agitation of protecting the rights of negroes".[147] While serving as a State Representative, he sponsored legislation to protect African American citizens against all avenues of discrimination.[148] By 1901, he had established and been elected President of the Afro-American Republican State League for Illinois.[149,150] His civic activity was stellar.

---

[146] Nashville Journal (Illinois), August 30, 1895, p.1
[147] The Altamont News, August 29, 1895, p.2
[148] Williams, Erma Brooks, Political Empowerment of Illinois' African American State Lawmakers from 1877 to 2005, University Press of America, 2008, p.5
[149] The Bystander, December 27, 1901, p.1
[150] The Rock Island Argus, March 8, 1902, p.1

In June of 1903, he drove an effort to impeach officials in St. Clair County, Illinois for allowing the release, lynching and burning of W.T. Wyatt in Belleville, Illinois by a murderous mob. Wyatt, a teacher, was accused of shooting the Charles Hertal, Superintendent of St. Clair County Schools, for not renewing his certificate.[151,152] These represent the tip of the iceberg but are overlooked because of the way he handled himself in all circles.

Jones published a severe public criticism of Booker T. Washington hinting at hypocrisy just prior to his expulsion from Freemasonry in 1903 in the same manner as he attacked Dr. Daniel Hale Williams and Provident Hospital. President of the Afro-American Equal Rights League at the time, he authored a resolution calling Washington a "turncoat" and further stating "above all things we regret that, while Booker T. Washington has advised the negro to refrain from politics, he himself has left the high plane of educator to aid in the appointment to

---

[151] Monroe County, Iowa:1901-1915, Iowa Genealogical Society, 1991, p.21
[152] The Daily Democrat, June 22, 1903, p.2

office of some of the most threadbare and discredited turncoats in the negro race."[153] Ire like this was unapologetically expressed to the world through the press.

National Negro Business League circa 1900
(Sumner Furniss standing on the left end, T.W. Jones standing on the right end, Dr. Daniel H. Williams seated next to Booker t. Washington on the left)

Blood brother or fraternal crony made no difference to Jones. Oddly enough, his brother, Theodore Wellington Jones was a member of Washington's Tuskegee Institute Executive Council and President of the Chicago Branch of Washington's National Negro Business League (NNBL). He

---

[153] The Inter Ocean, October 13, 1903, p.1

was a natural selection for leadership of the Chicago Branch because he promoted the types of policies supported by the NNBL before its inception when he served as a Cook County Commissioner in 1894.[154] Although the primary objective of the NNBL was to encourage colored citizens to enter all avenues of business, the cord it struck with Jones was that it tended to focus on doing so in a segregated fashion.[155] This was the likely cause of familial disputes in later years.

Jones destroyed his former crony William Gray after succeeding him as Grand Master of St. John's Grand Lodge. He expelled Gray in 1907 for supposed un-Masonic conduct along with John A. Bell. Both were expelled from all of the bodies under Jones' control.[156] He published in the "News from Chicago" section of the Montana Plaindealer in May of 1908: [157]

> *"Rev. Wm. Gray, of this city, who has made so much talk about building a home for the aged Baptist*

---

[154] The Broad Ax, April 9, 1904, p.1
[155] Asheville Citizen-Times, August 23, 1900, p.7
[156] The Washington Bee, January 19, 1907, p.5
[157] The Montana Plaindealer, May 1, 1908, p.1

> Ministers is now out of a church himself. Rev. Gray is
> unpopular with the people, nobody wants anything
> to do with him it is reported that he will soon leave
> the city and go to the Philippine Island and a large
> number of colored people in this city will be very glad
> when he takes his departure."

Jones attacked Gray for the same reasons he attacked Dr.
Daniel Hale Williams and Provident Hospital. Gray sought
to open a Kindergarten for negro children in 1905 and
continued to espouse other such innovations in a
segregated manner.[158] He also published articles defaming
Gray's efforts to try to establish a retirement facility for
aged ministers. In 1907, he published:[159]

> "The colored people in Chicago are very much
> astonished and surprised to think that the colored
> ministers of the Baptist convention that lately met in
> New Orleans, La., should have given their sanction
> and approval to any kind of a scheme that is

---

[158] The Inter Ocean, March 22, 1905, p.3
[159] The Statesman, August 2, 1907

engineered and directed by one William Gray of Chicago, who claims to be a minister of a Baptist church in Chicago. We are unable to find the church in the city of Chicago that he has charge of. The scheme of one Rev. William Gray is that he is attempting to collect money for building a home for aged colored Baptist ministers at Braidwood, Illinois, which is about 40 miles from Chicago. This is the same Rev. William Gray that has drifted around from place to place and a short time ago was compelled to leave Evanston, Ill., under the most unfavorable circumstances. This is the same Rev. Wm. Gray who was lately expelled from the Masonic fraternity in the state of Illinois."

Further angst was stoked when Gray led a coalition of ministers who sought to block Roosevelt and Taft from the Republican ticket in March of 1908.[160] A stalwart Republican leader, Jones vehemently opposed this stance which led to the aforementioned commentary in May of the

---

[160] Herald News, March 30, 1908, p.2

same year. The loss of Gray's congregation was subsequently published in non-congenial terms by Jones in the Montana Plaindealer in September of the same year:[161]

> *"Rev. William Gray who got a lot of cheap advertisement a short time ago by pretending to organize a home at Braidwood, Ill. for infirmed and aged Baptist ministers, has closed his church on State St which had a congregation of five persons and has got a job of work earning an honest dollar."*

Without mercy, Jones publicly scolded him, laid out his demise for the world to see, and basked in his downfall.

This explains why Jones may have been overlooked in many legitimate Masonic circles. The tenet of brotherly love or showing tolerance and respect for others' opinions was not his strong suit. Publicly railing against brothers who stood on the opposite sides of an issue was commonplace for him. While relief was provided through labors to protect the rights of African American citizens in the civic and legal arenas, it was not necessarily given in the same manner to

---

[161] Montana Plaindealer, September 11, 1908

brethren. Masonic opportunities in this area appear to have been performed for support in personal elevation.

Truth, in Freemasonry, is a core tenet. Earnestly striving for truth is not only a journey against moral turpitude but also for acceptance of reality. He fell short in this area as proven by the multiple avenues taken to achieve and hold on to power. For example, Jones had the following published along with an illustration of his likeness on the front page The Broad Ax in 1904:[162]

> *"A resolution was adopted that the Most Worshipful St. John's Grand Lodge of Illinois, of which Wm. Gray is Grand Master, and John G. Jones is Grand Secretary, is the only genuine and lawful colored Grand Lodge of A.F. and A. masons in the State of Illinois; and that the Grand Lodge that H.E. Burris is Grand Master of in the State of Illinois is a clandestine and bogus body and is not entitled to be recognized by any legitimate body of Masons in the world."*

---

[162] The Broad Ax, July 23, 1904, p.1

He further added that: [163]

> "...the Prince Hall Grand Lodge of Massachusetts
> that B.C. Hazen is styled as Grand Master of was a
> clandestine and unlawful Grand Lodge..."

Even further, he fully endorsed the following statement published in the Natchez Democrat in 1907 by Captain W.T. Grant, Deputy District Grand Master of the St. John's Grand Lodge: [164]

> "Prince Hall was an unlawful Mason and that he did
> not receive a charter from the Grand Lodge of
> England that was organized in the year 926 or any
> other Grand Lodge from the European Country"

Full endorsement of this statement with full knowledge of its inaccuracy was shameful. Overall, it is very difficult to present and accept the truth when ego is in the way.

So, what was Jones' real aim in Freemasonry in the 20th Century? Was it to open a small shop for business or

---

[163] The Broad Ax, July 23, 1904, p.1
[164] Natchez Democrat, March 8, 1907, p.4

execute a large-scale coup over an existing enterprise? The issuance of circulars of a split in the Grand Lodge was certainly a coup attempt. So was the attempt in the Scottish Rite. When those failed, he attempted to corrupt the foundation of Freemasonry and rebuild it in his own image but did so using sub-standard materials.

Jones' substitute for the cement of brotherly love was the hot lava and venom of hatred and revenge. For him, the legal environment was on his side. Any organization can incorporate and name itself as it sees fit. Municipalities are agnostic and will not legislate internal fraternal matters. This was proven in the 1880 suit between Prince Hall Consistory and the Supreme Council for the United States. So, an attorney of Jones' skill could easily leverage that argument to his benefit.

His substitute for solid stone bricks was little more than rocks, mud and spit fused together for a temporary patch. Several men often utter the phrase "once a Mason, always a Mason." This statement could not be further from the truth. A brother can lose his Masonic privileges which includes being called a "Mason". If suspended, is he still a brother? If expelled, is he still a brother? There answer is an emphatic "no!" By all accounts, he is no longer considered a Mason.

What kind of brother does not live up to his obligations? If life's challenges present conflicts, the altar is always available. Are there bad apples in Freemasonry? Yes, Jones himself is an example of this. Brethren of this caliber weaken the order and, if not redeemed, will become cancerous, expose the patches of rocks and spit, and cause the walls to fold.

His substitute for the virtues of Freemasonry were wounded pride and schemes. The offering of fraudulent degrees appears to be sourced from vengeance and a scheme to form a world of his own. His activities in Massachusetts confirmed this and they dealt with him accordingly.[165] Galivanting and consorting with bogus Masons in that locale assisting them in organizing and forming Lodges was a brazen effort. Emboldening John A.

---

[165] Proceedings, Most Worshipful Grand Lodge, AFAM, IL, 1904,p.126

Bell and others to do the same in Michigan was a clear violation of legitimate Masonic principles.[166]

One can easily see the expulsion of Jones as his primary impetus for instigating chaos. That train of poisonous thoughts apparently grew more potent in the company of like minds. From this catalyst, Grand Lodges of Self and self-made Grand Masters were born.

---

[166] The Broad Ax, July 23, 1904, p.1

4

Chapter Four:
PROFILE ASSESSMENTS

So, what is the assessment of John G. Jones in Freemasonry? Was he just a "hurt" person who decided to hurt other people? His profile certainly fits closely to that of a psychopath. According to Willem H.J. Martens in "The Hidden Suffering of a Psychopath", psychopathy is characterized: [167]

---

[167] Martens, Willem H.J., The Hidden Suffering of the Psychopath, Psychiatric Times, Vol. 19 No.1

"by diagnostic features such as superficial charm, high intelligence, poor judgment and failure to learn from experience, pathological egocentricity and incapacity for love, lack of remorse or shame, impulsivity, grandiose sense of self-worth, pathological lying, manipulative behavior, poor self-control, promiscuous sexual behavior, juvenile delinquency, and criminal versatility, among others."

While Marten's definition is quite extensive, many of these characteristics do certainly fit the personality of John G. Jones.

High intelligence and superficial charm are clear qualities that Jones possessed. He was the 8th black citizen admitted to the Illinois BAR and was able to garner support for many of his initiatives through his words.[168] He was highly respected in the legal arena which led to several social and civic elevations. His election to the Illinois

---

[168] Michigan Law Journal, Vol. 5, Dennis & Company, 1896, pp.386-390

General Assembly as a Republican in 1900 is a highlight to his climb in politics by way of his intelligence.

On the downside, while he was able to attract attention, he was not unable to sustain it due to poor judgment particularly in the Masonic ranks. Being removed or replaced from office became a common occurrence as a result. Its recurrence in the Grand Lodge, Scottish Rite and Shrine provides evidence that either he never learned from prior experiences or that he had grown cold hearted choosing to move forward despite the conflicts. Since he was intelligent and resourceful, the latter seems to better fit the bill.

While he clearly expressed a pathological egocentricity, there isn't enough evidence to support the idea that he lacked the capacity for love. He believed wholeheartedly in everything that he did even during times where he was clearly wrong. Claiming ignorance on the legitimacy of the Grand Lodge of Illinois was an outright lie. So was the claim of illegitimacy of the USC-SJ under Sovereign Grand Commander Thornton Jackson. So, he was willing to cross lines of morality to achieve a goal. This shows that love of self was more important than morals.

While this display of pathological behavior was done for selfish reasons, it does not conclude that he was incapable of love. It proves that his concept of love was limited to those things that he felt were of the utmost importance to him which did include the African American community in general. He took hard stances taken to secure rights of African American citizens under the law. In all instances, he felt he was equal to any person and didn't need special treatment to succeed. For this love, he'd fight to the death.

But brotherly love, on the other hand, in the Masonic sense, was lacking to a large degree. It fell short as personal gain appeared to trump all other things. To be the "first" or "most powerful" was the aim. The concept of service in these circles seemed to conflict with ego.

The bulk of his labors were clearly manipulative in the realm of Freemasonry. His sense of self-worth was overblown. He labelled himself "the greatest Afro-

American Mason in the world" in several articles in the Broad Ax and often published in third person. For example, he noted in an 1899 edition of the Broad Ax "John G. Jones, the greatest Afro-American Mason in the world, has returned home from his sojourn in Denver, Colorado, the Queen City of the West."[169] Months later in the same paper he is touted as "the highest Afro-American Mason in the world".[170] The trend repeated itself as he again labeled himself "the greatest Afro-American Mason in the world" on the front page of the December 28, 1901 edition of the Broad Ax.[171]

The need for self-aggrandizement particularly in a publication for which he was, himself, an editor is a clear indicator that he had a grandiose sense of self-worth. But, the continual promotion by others under his control made them enablers to the madness. So, he was not alone in his quest for power, he had help.

---

[169] The Broad Ax, December 23, 1899, p.1
[170] The Broad Ax, July 28, 1900, p.1
[171] The Broad Ax, December 28, 1901, p.1

Puffing oneself up through surreptitious means is also an indicator of a poor sense of self-control. Is it moral to blatantly lie about the legitimacy of an organization that was contrived by way of a lie? How can one claim humility and decency while puffing himself up publicly through a manipulation of the truth? While it wreaks of egotism, it also wreaks of an inferiority complex.

Also, for every boast of fame or fortune presented by Jones, there was a more truthful backstory somewhere. He bragged about being the highest or greatest Afro-American Mason in the world as a defense mechanism because he had been stomped by multiple bodies. Hurt people do hurt other people but a line had to be drawn in the sand to end it.

One point that has not been addressed is finances. Trust in leadership and administration was a shortcoming for Jones particularly in his efforts to inculcated Masons with degrees from the first to the thirty-third along with York Rite degrees. The accounting of the finances appeared to be a major point of contention particularly with those who split from the Jones organizations. The high skepticism about funds and their final destinations were warranted. James A. Farrier, Dorsey Seville and others certainly questioned this. Even though Seville questioned it while under duress from Jones' attacks, the point relative to a lack of financial accounting from the Office of the Imperial Grand Potentate was still valid. Jones responded with no response and continued to operate as he saw fit.

That being said, should a narcissistic, ego-manic be considered trustworthy with funds? Would a dictator really give a true and accurate account of his spending to people whom he felt were beneath him? Most likely, no.

Another question is, how was Jones able to operate in the manner that he did without providing a sufficient financial report? Were Nobles too afraid to challenge him or did many folks have hands in the pot? Even though Seville provided details on receipts and expenses, his actions in support of Jones through the years and willingness to vigorously defend him increases the likelihood that even he was not completely truthful when he published his finances in The Washington Bee. A staunch Jones follower, he was probably guilty by association but was definitely a mark that Jones exploited to the fullest and tossed away when he was done.

OVERVIEW OF THE DISC THEORY

These characteristics provide a clear profile of the type of personality intrinsic to John G. Jones. His historical behaviors have been weighed against the 1928 DISC Emotional and Behavioral Theory by psychologist William Moulton Marston. According to Marston's theory, evaluations fall in the following four categories which can provide insights into personality types:[172]

- **Type D: Dominance** (Red)
  - *Mode:* Active or Outgoing
  - *Orientation:* Task Driven
  - *Positives:* Direct, Decisive, Doers
  - *Negatives:* Domineering, Demanding

---

[172] Eikenberry, Kevin, Guy Harris, From Bud to Boss: Secrets to a Successful Transition to Remarkable Leadership, Wiley, 2011, pp.115-116

- **Type I:** **Influence** (Yellow)
  - *Mode:* Active or Outgoing
  - *Orientation:* People Driven
  - *Positives:* Inspirational, Interactive, Interesting
  - *Negatives:* Impulsive, Irritating
- **Type S:** **Steadiness** (Green)
  - *Mode*: Reflective and Reserved
  - *Orientation*: People Driven
  - *Positives:* Stable, Supportive, Sincere
  - *Negatives:* Slow and Sensitive
- **Type C:** **Compliance** (Blue):
  - *Mode:* Reflective and Reserved
  - *Orientation:* Task Driven
  - *Positives:* Cautious, Careful, Conscientious
  - *Negatives:* Calculating, Condescending

DISC PROFILE ASSESSMENT – JOHN G. JONES

An evaluation of Jones revealed that he was a Type D.[173] He actively utilized force to overcome resistance in the environment and implement his plans. Although he did exhibit positive qualities including being direct, decisive, and a doer, his negative qualities of being domineering and demanding were more dominant. Tendencies of this personality type include: [174]

---

[173] Onlinedisctests.com, IQTEST INSTITUTE, evaluated 12/31/2022
[174] https://discinsights.com/personality-style-d, retrieved 12/2/2022

- tend to focus on the big picture and will step over authority to desired achieve results;
- prefer to be in charge and crave control out of the fear of being taken advantage of by others;
- desire freedom from the rules of others and continually seeks opportunities for advancement.

Furthermore, this personality type wants to:

"look forward and think in more significant terms, they tend to ignore the information and analysis of past experiences and the details of what new projects may entail. They may ignore potential risks, not weigh the pros and cons, and not consider others' opinions. They will likely offer innovative and progressive ideas and systems but will need someone else to break down the project and work with the specifics."

Jones' historical track record confirms these results.

DISC PROFILE ASSESSMENT – DORSEY F. SEVILLE

An evaluation of Dorsey F. Seville revealed that he was a Type S.[175] His primary focus seemed to be on service for the cause. He continually showed blind loyalty to the aims and objectives of Jones. It was his home where the Bogus Supreme Council was created. It was from his pen that the exploits of Jones were reported through various media across the nation and beyond. Although he produced some works that were inspirational (his articles), his devotion to Jones confirms that he was a people pleaser

---

[175] Onlinedisctests.com, IQTEST INSTITUTE, evaluated 12/31/2022

and somewhat reserved as It relates to expressing his opinions. Before severing ties with Jones, he admitted the spurious nature of the creation of that Bogus Supreme Council and performed the desired tasks knowing that they were wrong.

DISC PROFILE ASSESSMENT – RICHARD E. MOORE

An evaluation of Richard E. Moore revealed that he was a Type C.[176] He was an analytical thinker and systematic in his approach to decision making. He is the longest-tenured, elected Grand Lodge Officer in the history of the

---

[176] Onlinedisctests.com, IQTEST INSTITUTE, evaluated 12/31/2022

Most Worshipful Prince Hall Grand Lodge of Illinois as Grand Secretary for more than thirty years. He also served in this position while serving as Grand Secretary and Recorder for other bodies and the chief executive officer of others. He was not a slow decision maker but was steady in his avenues of service. He worked within the defined boundaries to achieve tasks but was also a calculating character who was able to successfully maneuver through the challenges pressed by Jones. He, however, did submit to Milton Fields not only within the Scottish Rite but also within the Shrine. From all historical accounts, locally and nationally, there is no mud on his name only laurels for his stability and accomplishments.

The relationship between the Moore Brothers and James W. Taylor also re-affirms the Type C personality of Richard E. Moore. As Grand Master, Taylor implemented sweeping changing to the administration of the Grand Lodge of Illinois. He is credited with the introduction of forms and standardization of administrative processes in the early stages of the Grand Lodge that Richard implemented as Grand Secretary. This indicates that he and

Moore were kindred Type C spirits and able to work together seamlessly. This simplification of the entire operational processes of the Grand Lodge transferred well through the leadership term of Joseph W. Moore.

There is no indication of strain in the relationship between Richard and Most Worshipful Brother Joseph W. Moore. During his term of leadership, Joseph moved forward without a hitch. Richard had been Grand Secretary for several years by the time of his installation so the finances and function of the Grand Lodge went smoothly.

Joseph's personality aligned more with Type I. He was. Most definitely, a "people" person who was a very effective communicator. He did not appear as a dictator but leveraged situations to inspire loyalty and support. His suspension of Jones in 1887 showed strength. His reinstatement of Jones, despite the fact that a law suit was involved, showed mercy. But not fully closing the door on Jones at the time, the show of mercy, is a clear indicator that he was not a Type D personality.

DISC PROFILE ASSESSMENT – MILTON F. FIELDS

An evaluation of Milton F. Fields revealed that he and Jones were more alike than different. He was a Type I.[177] Although he was domineering, he was more of a people-person than Jones which is the defining difference between the two. After being expelled from the legitimate Scottish Rite Body, he started his own drawing men of like character into his circle. His impulsive nature was what drew him to immediately create a Shrine Faction of his own mirroring Jones.

---

[177] Onlinedisctests.com, IQTEST INSTITUTE, evaluated 12/31/2022

The evidence of Fields' superior people skills is that he was not seen as a dictator in the eyes of his followers. As his people skills eventually fell short to his impulsive nature, he acquiesced. He took the humble route particularly within the Shrine by taking the Oath of Fealty to the AEAONMS. His humility led to the exaltation of being classified as a Past Imperial Potentate of the AEAONMS. This is the final differentiating factor for the selection of the DISC types between him and Jones. Fields did humble himself while Jones never even considered it.

There is no "best" profile type for leadership. Successful leaders typically balance out teams and leverage diversity to obtain the best methods to move organizations forward. Jones, Moore, Seville and Fields did realize degrees of success in their various organizations but their lasting impressions vary due to the manner in which their personalities reverberated. Moore's legacy is one of honor and nobility. Fields' lasting impression was redemptive. Seville's legacy is akin to that of a blind follower even though he did finally expose the truth. The negative legacy of Jones, however, can be summarized in one word – "indignation".

Yet, to have achieved individual successes confirmed that their styles were conducive, for a time in some cases, to the environments under their control. Positive or negative, their actions and impacts still reverberate in the modern era. As such, their examples provide great food for thought that should be leveraged by current and future leaders.

5

Chapter Five:

FOOD FOR THOUGHT

All in all, the entire set of circumstances surrounding Jones makes one wonder what could have been had he absorbed the concept of actually being "Worshipful" as noted in the Holy Bible: [178]

> "If my people, which are called by name, shall humble themselves, and pray, and seek my face, and

---

[178] The Holy Bible, 2 Chronicles 7:14

> turn from their wicked ways; then will I hear from
> heaven, and will forgive their sin, and will heal their
> land."

His brother, Theodore Wellington Jones, did this which repaired and secured a strong Masonic legacy in the diaspora of Freemasonry. He remained active in the Masonic ranks well after his brother's expulsion and did not join the bogus Grand Lodge. If Jones had sought this path, maybe things would have gone differently. Instead, he created the quintessential ball of confusion which resulted in bogus Freemasonry.

While the term bogus Freemasonry can encompass the whole diaspora of the Order, Jones' influence had a heavy impact on Symbolic Masonry. When rebuffed by legitimate Grand Lodges, he turned to W.D. Matthews and the National Grand Lodge. His intent, though, was to absorb Grand Lodes under the Scottish Rite so that he could retain full control. The publications in public media about his treatment by the Grand Lodge of Illinois still reverberate as sympathy fodder today and are utilized by some to justify the continuance of bogus organizations. But his actions, laid a pathway for others to indoctrinate an impure version of Freemasonry onto others perpetuating the system of bogus Masonry that still infects today.

The St. John's Grand Lodge established by Jones and Gray does still exist in the State of Illinois. While many of its membership consists of good men, the sources of the organization are two expelled Prince Hall Masons by the name of John G. Jones and Rev. William Gray. Some members may be well aware of this fact while others have no clue. Yet, the symbols and name of Freemasonry are a part of that organization and being utilized, although illegitimately, to promote a Masonic dogma that is impure. However, as they perform the same tasks in communities as recognized Masons do, there may be a chance for reconciliation, to heal that wound opened by an ego-manic and his crony over a century ago.

The St. James Grand Lodge organized in 1936 after splitting from the St. John's Grand Lodge due to factional segregation. It followed the pattern that was set by the formation of its predecessor. [179] In doing so, it reaffirmed the method that many of the thousands of organizations now utilize in today's era to start Grand Lodges.

The First St. John's Grand Lodge is sourced from the same stock. It also organized itself in the same way. Its membership pales in comparison to the others but the challenge still remains. The method that was introduced to create an independent Masonic organization was incorrect. While they may wear the emblems, they are not true practitioners because their link to legitimacy is not intact.

Many other organizations followed the same process in Illinois and beyond. According to the Joseph A. Walkes Jr. Commission on Bogus Masonic Practices of the Phylaxis Society, there are hundreds more.[180] Some expanded with earnest intent under the belief that separation was acceptable and in accord with Masonic standards. Others were intentionally spurious. All in all, the

---

[179] https://mwsjgl.org/history.html, retrieved December 23, 2022
[180] https://thephylaxis.org/bogus/bogus-organizations.html, retrieved December 23, 2022

scourge which was exploded by Jones has replicated itself across the nation and remains a problem today.

The reality is that men who joined organizations like these were most likely unaware of the truth. Many of them are excellent citizens in their respective communities and prominent in business, civic and political circles. As such, it is of the utmost importance for members of organizations who can trace themselves back to legitimate roots to make concerted efforts to get the history documented and into their hands. It would be beneficial to do the opposite of what Jones would do and actually host conversations on the topic. Doing nothing will allow the same actions to repeat themselves in the future. So, communication, can produce a pathway of restoration onto the chain hoop of legitimacy.

Masonic principles endorse this solution. Forward-thinking individuals should be proactive and reach out with an olive branch of friendship instead of Jones' scimitar of death. The manner of communication may be the factor that causes someone to seek to be healed. This will provide a path for the erection of a new legacy of symmetry.

So, what is the final Masonic legacy of John G. Jones? It is the story of a quick rise and a hard fall of a man with potential who could not overcome his own vanity, pride, and egotism. His wounded pride drove him down a pathway of degradation away from Masonic principles which led to his doom. While he did achieve some positives, he disgraced himself with his selfish, short-term actions which opened Pandora's box of Bogus Masonry. May his legacy be the line below which Masons choose not to sink. For short-term achievement may provide immediate joy, it can cause harm in the long run. As such, Masons must be on guard to protect the fraternity from the mistakes of the past so that they do not rear their ugly heads in the paths of the future.

Afterword

The profile of Jones should be studied and utilized as a tool to improve awareness of the different personality types that exist in organizations. The examples shown herein have provided a pattern and indicators that members should consider when lining up leaders of the future. Awareness of the personality types can help leaders determine the best modes of communication to achieve the desired organizational goals.

In reviewing the circumstances surrounding Jones, his peers and his opponents, he was somewhat successful in achieving short term goals but failed to sustain leadership over long haul due to his conflicting personality traits. However, had he practiced the true tenets of Freemasonry, he may have been fully successful. Brotherly love, relief and truth are not meant to be utilized only for short term solutions or quick wins but long-term strategies of respect for mutual success. Their practice become even more critical for the survival of the fraternity.

Violations against the tenets must be enforced immediately. They can first be whispered in the ear of an ill-acting brother and escalated further if no heed is taken after the initial address. Fear of doing so often equates to the continuance of behaviors that are unbecoming of Masons which can destroy the core of Lodges from the inside out.

There is definitely a sense of duty associated with brotherly love that must be fulfilled for posterity. How can one sincerely proclaim it without putting it into action. While love is a noun, it can also be a verb. Its utilization is the motion that provides relief when a brother is in need. It is the substance of humanity that drives one to speak truth not only to power but also to one another on equal ground. Acceptance of the fact that no man is greater than another ensures that the master/slave spectrum never enters the fold. In doing so, all can meet and act on the same plain and part squarely as men.

Appendices

Appendix A:
JONES TIMELINE (1871 -1903)

Year	House	Event
1871	Lodge	Raised a Master Mason of John Jones Lodge #7, Chicago, Illinois
1872	Lodge	Appointed Senior Deacon of John Jones Lodge #7, Chicago, Illinois
1873	Lodge	Elected Senior Warden of John Jones Lodge #7, Chicago, Illinois
1873	Grand Lodge	Elected Grand Secretary of the Grand Lodge for 1873-74

1874	Grand Lodge	Re-elected Grand Secretary of the Grand Lodge for 1874-75
1875	Grand Lodge	Elected Deputy Grand Master of the Grand Lodge for 1875-76
1875	Grand Lodge	Appointed District Deputy Grand Master of the First District
1876	Lodge	Elected Worshipful Master of John Jones Lodge #7, Chicago, Illinois
1876	Grand Lodge	LOST election for Grand Master of the Grand Lodge for 1876-77
1877	Grand Lodge	Offered Resolution for the Grand Lodge to withdraw from the National Grand Lodge (Compact)
1879	Grand Lodge	LOST election for Grand Master of the Grand Lodge for 1879-80
1879	Scottish Rite	Organized Prince Hall Consistory of Chicago, Illinois under the Supreme Council for the Southern and Western Jurisdiction (SC-SWJ) Charter Grand Secretary of Prince Hall Consistory of Chicago, Illinois
1880	Scottish Rite	Filed suit against the Supreme Council for the United States (USSC) to prevent expansion in the City of Chicago Re-elected Grand Secretary of Prince Hall Consistory of Chicago, Illinois
1880	Holy Royal Arch Masons	Charter Excellent High Priest of Eureka Chapter #3 of Chicago, Illinois
1881	Scottish Rite	Re-elected Grand Secretary of Prince Hall Consistory of Chicago, Illinois
1881	Holy Royal Arch Masons	Re-elected Excellent High Priest of Eureka Chapter #3 of Chicago, Illinois
1882	Scottish Rite	Re-elected Grand Secretary of Prince Hall Consistory of Chicago, Illinois

1883	Scottish Rite	Elected Grand Auditor General (SC-SWJ)
		Deputy for Illinois, Indiana, Kansas, Arkansas, Colorado, and Minnesota;
		Re-elected Grand Secretary of Prince Hall Consistory of Chicago, Illinois
1884	Scottish Rite	Grand Auditor General (SC-SWJ)
		Deputy for Illinois, Indiana, Kansas, Arkansas, Colorado, and Minnesota;
		Re-elected Grand Secretary of Prince Hall Consistory of Chicago, Illinois
1885	Scottish Rite	Grand Auditor General (SC-SWJ)
		Deputy for Illinois, Indiana, Kansas, Arkansas, Colorado, and Minnesota;
		Re-elected Grand Secretary of Prince Hall Consistory of Chicago, Illinois
1886	Scottish Rite	Grand Auditor General (SC-SWJ)
		Deputy for Illinois, Indiana, Kansas, Arkansas, Colorado, and Minnesota;
		Re-elected Grand Secretary of Prince Hall Consistory of Chicago, Illinois
1887	Knights Templar	Elected Eminent Commander of Corinthian Commandery #1 of Chicago, Illinois
1887	Grand Lodge	Suspended from Freemasonry
		Reinstated in October of 1887
1887	Scottish Rite	Deputy for Illinois, Indiana, Kansas, Arkansas, Colorado, and Minnesota;
		Re-elected Grand Secretary of Prince Hall Consistory of Chicago, Illinois (USC-SJ)

1888	Knights Templar	Elected Eminent Commander of Corinthian Commandery #1 of Chicago, Illinois
1888	Scottish Rite	Grand Auditor General (USC-SJ) Deputy for Illinois, Indiana, Kansas, Arkansas, Colorado, and Minnesota; Re-elected Grand Secretary of Prince Hall Consistory of Chicago, Illinois
1889	Knights Templar	Elected Eminent Commander of Corinthian Commandery #1 of Chicago, Illinois
1889	Scottish Rite	Elected Lieutenant Grand Commander (USC-SJ) Deputy for Indiana; Re-elected Grand Secretary of Prince Hall Consistory of Chicago, Illinois
1890	Knights Templar	Elected Eminent Commander of Corinthian Commandery #1 of Chicago, Illinois
1890	Scottish Rite	Lieutenant Grand Commander (USC-SJ) Deputy for Illinois, Kansas, Arkansas, Colorado, and Minnesota; Re-elected Grand Secretary of Prince Hall Consistory of Chicago, Illinois
1891	Scottish Rite	Lieutenant Grand Commander (USC-SJ) Deputy for Illinois, Kansas, Arkansas, Colorado, and Minnesota; Re-elected Grand Secretary of Prince Hall Consistory of Chicago, Illinois

1892	Scottish Rite	Lieutenant Grand Commander (USC-SJ)
		Deputy for Illinois, Kansas, Arkansas, Colorado, and Minnesota;
		Re-elected Grand Secretary of Prince Hall Consistory of Chicago, Illinois
1893	Scottish Rite	Lieutenant Grand Commander (USC-SJ)
		Deputy for Illinois, Kansas, Arkansas, Colorado, and Minnesota;
		Re-elected Grand Secretary of Prince Hall Consistory of Chicago, Illinois
1893	Shrine	Received Shrine Degrees from Noble Rofeldt Ali Pasha
		Organized the Imperial Grand Council, Ancient Arabic Order Nobles of the Mystic Shrine (AAONMS)
		First Imperial Grand Potentate
1894	Cryptic Rite	Organized the General Grand Council of Royal and Select Masters
		First Most Illustrious Grand Master
1894	Shrine	Imperial Grand Potentate
1894	Scottish Rite	Lieutenant Grand Commander (USC-SJ)
		Deputy for Illinois, Kansas, Arkansas, Colorado, and Minnesota;
		Re-elected Grand Secretary of Prince Hall Consistory of Chicago, Illinois
1895	Shrine	Imperial Grand Potentate
1895	Cryptic Rite	Most Illustrious Grand Master

1895	Scottish Rite	Lieutenant Grand Commander (USC-SJ)
		Deputy for Illinois, Kansas, Arkansas, Colorado, and Minnesota;
		Re-elected Grand Secretary of Prince Hall Consistory of Chicago, Illinois
1895	Scottish Rite	Lieutenant Grand Commander (USC-SJ)
		LOST election for Sovereign Grand Commander (USC-SJ)
		Expelled from USC-SJ
		Organized Bogus United Supreme Council for the Southern and Western Jurisdiction
		First Sovereign Grand Commander of Bogus Supreme Council
1896	Allied Masonic Degrees	Charter Deputy Grand Master of the Sovereign College of Allied Masonic Degrees
1896	Shrine	Imperial Grand Potentate
1896	Cryptic Rite	Most Illustrious Grand Master
1896	Scottish Rite BOGUS	Incorporated Bogus United Supreme Council for the Southern and Western Jurisdiction
		Elected Sovereign Grand Commander of Bogus Supreme Council
		Incorporated Prince Hall Consistory under the Bogus Supreme Council
1897	Allied Masonic Degrees	Deputy Grand Master of the Sovereign College of Allied Masonic Degrees
1897	Shrine	Imperial Grand Potentate

1897	Cryptic Rite	Most Illustrious Grand Master
1897	Scottish Rite BOGUS	Sovereign Grand Commander of Bogus Supreme Council
1898	Allied Masonic Degrees	Sovereign Grand Master of the Sovereign College of Allied Masonic Degrees
1898	Shrine	Imperial Grand Potentate
1898	Cryptic Rite	Most Illustrious Grand Master
1898	Scottish Rite BOGUS	Sovereign Grand Commander of Bogus Supreme Council
1899	Allied Masonic Degrees	Sovereign Grand Master of the Sovereign College of Allied Masonic Degrees
1899	Shrine	Imperial Grand Potentate
1899	Cryptic Rite	Most Illustrious Grand Master
1899	Scottish Rite BOGUS	Sovereign Grand Commander of Bogus Supreme Council
1900	Allied Masonic Degrees	Sovereign Grand Master of the Sovereign College of Allied Masonic Degrees
1900	Shrine	Imperial Grand Potentate
1900	Cryptic Rite	Most Illustrious Grand Master
1900	Scottish Rite BOGUS	Sovereign Grand Commander of Bogus Supreme Council
1901	Allied Masonic Degrees	Sovereign Grand Master of the Sovereign College of Allied Masonic Degrees
1901	Shrine	Imperial Grand Potentate
1901	Cryptic Rite	Most Illustrious Grand Master
1901	Scottish Rite BOGUS	Sovereign Grand Commander of Bogus Supreme Council

1902	Allied Masonic Degrees	Sovereign Grand Master of the Sovereign College of Allied Masonic Degrees
1902	Shrine	Imperial Grand Potentate
1902	Cryptic Rite	Most Illustrious Grand Master
1902	Scottish Rite BOGUS	Sovereign Grand Commander of Bogus Supreme Council
1903	Allied Masonic Degrees	Sovereign Grand Master of the Sovereign College of Allied Masonic Degrees
1903	Shrine	Imperial Grand Potentate
1903	Cryptic Rite	Most Illustrious Grand Master
1903	Scottish Rite BOGUS	Sovereign Grand Commander of Bogus Supreme Council

Appendix B:
AFRO-AMERICAN SUPREME COUNCILS

- **Supreme Council for the Northern Jurisdiction (King David/Darius)**
  - Organized in 1856 under the leadership of Illustrious David Leary
  - Headquarters in Philadelphia, Pennsylvania
  - <u>Retired</u> after consolidation in 1881 (USC-NJ)
- **Supreme Council for the United States (USSC)**
  - Organized in 1864 (Compact) by Illustrious Auguste Hugo De Bulow
  - Headquarters in New York, New York
  - <u>Retired</u> in 1893 after agreement with Milton Fields (SC-NWJ) – *see page 55*

- **Supreme Council for the Southern and Western Jurisdiction (SC-SWJ)**
  - Organized in 1869 under the leadership of Illustrious Thornton A. Jackson
  - Headquarters in Washington, District of Columbia
  - Retired after consolidation agreement in 1886 which was perfected in 1887 (USC-SJ)
- **Supreme Council for the Southern Jurisdiction (Star of Bethlehem)**
  - Organized in 1870 (Compact) under the leadership of Lemuel G. Griffin
  - Headquarters in Baltimore, Maryland
  - Retired after consolidation agreement in 1886 which was perfected in 1887 (USC-SJ)
- **King Frederick Supreme Council**
  - Organized in 1871 under the leadership of Joshua D. Kelley
  - Headquarters in Philadelphia, Pennsylvania
  - Retired after consolidation in 1881 (USC-NJ)

- **United Supreme Council, Ancient and Accepted Scottish Rite of Freemasonry, Northern Jurisdiction (USC-NJ)**
  - Organized in 1881 by consolidation agreement between King David and King Frederick Supreme Councils
  - Headquarters in Philadelphia, Pennsylvania
- **United Supreme Council, Ancient and Accepted Scottish Rite of Freemasonry, Southern Jurisdiction (USC-SJ)**
  - Organized in 1886 by consolidation agreement between SC-SWJ and Star of Bethlehem Supreme Councils
  - Headquarters in Memphis, Tennessee
- **Supreme Council for the Northern and Western Jurisdiction (SC-NWJ)**
  - Organized in 1893 as a spurious Supreme Council after the expulsion of Milton Fields from the USC-NJ and USC-SJ
  - Headquarters in St. Louis, Missouri
  - Retired after the death of Fields in 1917

- **United Supreme Council for the Southern and Western Jurisdiction (USC-SWJ)**
  - Organized in 1895 and incorporated in 1896 as a spurious Supreme Council after the expulsion of John G. Jones from the USC-SJ
  - Headquarters in Washington, D.C.
- **Supreme Council for the Northeastern Jurisdiction (SC-NEJ)**
  - Organized in 1896 as a spurious Supreme Council with the officers installed by Milton Fields, SC-NWJ
  - Headquarters in New York, New York
  - Presumed defunct

Appendix C:
PRIMARY IMPERIAL COUNCILS

- **Imperial Grand Council, Ancient Arabic Order of the Nobles of the Mystic Shrine of North and South America (AAONMS)**
    - John G. Jones received Shrine degrees from Noble Rofeldt Pasha on June 1, 1893
    - Organized the Imperial Grand Council on June 10, 1893 by John G. Jones in Chicago, Illinois by patent of authority issued by Noble Rofeldt Pasha of the Arabia Grand Council
    - Presumed spurious after reorganization in December of 1900 by Isaac L.W. Holland (AEAONMS)

- **Imperial Council for the United States and Canada, Ancient Arabic Order of the Nobles of the Mystic Shrine (AAONMS)**
  - Organized in March 24, 1894 by Milton Fields
  - Incorporated in Chicago, Illinois on August 3, 1894
  - <u>Retired</u> after Fields pledged fealty to the AEAONMS in 1911
- **Imperial Council, Ancient Egyptian Arabic Order of the Nobles of the Mystic Shrine (AEAONMS)**
  - Organized in 1900 by Isaac L.W. Holland
  - Incorporated November 1901 with incorporators listed as Robert D. Ruffin, Magnus L. Robinson, Jesse H. Foster, John H. Jones, Dabney Smith, Isaac L.W. Holland, C.A. Knox, J.W. Smothers and Edwin A. Turpin[181]

---

[181] Evening Star, November 19, 1901, p.3

Appendix D:
FACTIONS

Key Members of the Jones Faction

The Jones Faction refers to the primary supporters of John G. Jones through his ventures at the local, state-wide and national levels in Masonic and civic organizations.

- **Barnett, Ferdinand L.** (Chicago, Illinois)
  - Past Master of Hiram Lodge #14;
  - Past Senior Grand Warden, MWPHGL of Illinois;

- o 3rd black lawyer admitted to the Illinois BAR;
- o Law partner of Jones and Morris;
- o 1st black Illinois Assistant States Attorney;
- o owner of the Conservator Newspaper;
- o married Ida B. Wells

- **Bell, John A.** (Grand Rapids, Michigan)
  - o Founder of a BOGUS Grand Lodge;
  - o Founding member of the United Supreme Council for the Southern and Western Jurisdiction (BOGUS);
  - o Past Imperial Deputy Grand Potentate and Imperial Grand Recorder, AAONMS

- **Darrow, William L.** (Chicago, Illinois)
  - o Past Master of North Star Lodge #1;
  - o Past Grand Master of Illinois Prince Hall Masons; Member of Prince Hall Consistory (SC-SWJ and USC-SJ);
  - o Past Deputy for the Orient of Minnesota (USC-SJ);
  - o Past Most Excellent Grand High Priest of Illinois

- **Dempsey, Dillard W.** (Chicago, Illinois)
  - Past Master of John Jones Lodge #7;
  - Past Deputy Grand Master, MWPHGL of Illinois;
  - Past Deputy for the Orient of Illinois (USC-SJ);
  - Past Eminent Commander and Past Recorder, Corinthian Commandery #1;
  - Past Imperial Chief Rabban, AAONMS
- **Dunmore, John W.** (Chicago, Illinois)
  - Past Master of John Jones Lodge #7;
  - Past Grand Trustee, MWPHGL of Illinois;
  - Past Commander-In-Chief, Prince Hall Consistory (SC-SWJ and USC-SJ);
  - Past Deputy for the Orient of Kansas;
  - Past Grand Master of Ceremonies (USC-SJ);
  - Past Excellent High Priest, St. Marks Chapter #1, HRAM;
  - Past Grand Lecturer, MEPHGC HRAM (Illinois);

- o Past Eminent Commander, Corinthian Commandery #1, KT;
  - o Past Commander-In-Chief of Prince Hall Consistory;
  - o Past Imperial High Priest and Prophet, AAONMS

- **Gray, Rev. William** (Chicago, Illinois)
  - o Past Master of John Jones Lodge #7;
  - o Past Commander-In-Chief of Prince Hall Consistory (when BOGUS);
  - o Expelled Prince Hall Mason, 1904;
  - o Co-conspirator in establishment of St. John's Grand Lodge in Chicago (BOGUS);
  - o Former Mississippi State Legislator[182]

- **Hancock, Richard Mason** (Chicago, Illinois)
  - o Past Master of North Star Lodge #1;
  - o Past Senior Grand Warden and Past Grand Secretary, MWPHGL of Illinois;

---

[182] http://msstate-exhibits.libraryhost.com/exhibits/show/legislators/item/486

- o Past Commander-In-Chief of Prince Hall Consistory (SC-SWJ);

- o Past Deputy for the Orient of Wisconsin (USC-SJ)

- **Jones, John George** (Chicago, Illinois)
  - o Past Master of John Jones Lodge #7;
  - o Past Deputy Grand Master and Past Grand Secretary, MWPHGL of Illinois;
  - o Charter Grand Secretary and Past Grand Master (1906) of the St. Johns Grand Lodge (Bogus);
  - o Founder and Charter Imperial Grand Potentate, AAONMS;
  - o Charter Grand Secretary, Prince Hall Consistory (SC-SWJ);
  - o Past Lieutenant Grand Commander and Past Deputy for the Orients of Illinois, Indiana, Kansas, Arkansas, Colorado, and Minnesota (SC-SWJ and USC-SJ);
  - o Past Grand Auditor General and Past Deputy (SC-SWJ);

- o Charter Sovereign Grand Commander (Bogus USC-SWJ);
- o Charter Excellent High Priest, Eureka Chapter #3, HRAM;
- o Past Eminent Commander, Corinthian Commandery #1, KT;
- o Charter Most Illustrious Grand Master, General Grand Council, Cryptic Rite, Royal and Select Masters;
- o Charter Most Eminent Grand Master, General Grand Encampment, Knights Templar;
- o Charter Deputy Sovereign Master and Past Sovereign Grand Master, Allied Masonic Degrees for North America;
- o Past State Representative for the Illinois General Assembly (1900)

- **Jones, Theodore Wellington** (Chicago, Illinois)
  - o Brother of John G. Jones;
  - o Past Master of John Jones Lodge #7;
  - o Past Grand Lecturer, MWPHGL of Illinois;

- - Charter President, National Negro Business League, Chicago Branch
  - 2nd Black Cook County Commissioner (Illinois)
- **Matthews, Captain W.D.** (Leavenworth, Kansas)
  - Past National Grand Master of the Compact Grand Lodge
- **Morris, Edward H.** (Chicago, Illinois)
  - Member of John Jones Lodge #7;
  - renowned African American Attorney, 5th black attorney to be appointed to the Illinois BAR;
  - Law partner of Jones and Barnett
- **Newton, Rev. Charles W.** (Jacksonville, Illinois)
  - Member of St. John Lodge #8;[183]
  - Charter Sovereign Grand Master, Allied Masonic Degrees for North America;
  - prominent official in the African Methodist Episcopal Church

---

[183] Proceedings, Most Worshipful Grand Lodge, AFAM, IL, 1898, p.73

- **Rogers, Benjamin F.** (Springfield, Illinois)
  - Charter Grand Master of Illinois Prince Hall Masons;
  - Civic activist and former Conductor on the Underground Railroad in the State of Illinois
- **Seville, Dorsey F.** (Washington, D.C.)
  - Secretary General of the United Supreme Council for the Southern and Western Jurisdiction (BOGUS);
  - Imperial Grand Secretary and Imperial Grand Correspondence Secretary, AAONMS
- **Thomas, John W.E.** (Chicago, Illinois)
  - 1st black elected to the Illinois General Assembly and sponsor for the 1885 Civil Rights Act for the State of Illinois
- **Waring, Robert C.** (Chicago, Illinois)
  - Past Master of North Star Lodge #1;
  - Past Grand Secretary, MWPHGL of Illinois;
  - Past Deputy for the Orient of Michigan (USC-SJ);

- Past Commander-In-Chief, Occidental Consistory (SC-NWJ) after defecting from Jones Faction;
- Past Eminent Commander, Corinthian Commandery #1

- **Wheeler, Lloyd G.** (Chicago, Illinois)
  - 1st black attorney admitted to the Illinois BAR;
  - Son-in-law of John Jones, Past Grand Master of Ohio and uncle of John G. Jones

Key Members of the Moore Faction

The Moore Faction refers to the primary supporters of Richard E. Moore, his older brother Joseph W. Moore and James W. Taylor through their ventures at the local, state-wide and national levels in Masonic and civic organizations.

- **Burris, Henry E.** (Rock Island, Illinois)
  - Past Master of King Solomon Lodge #20;
  - Past Grand Master of Illinois Prince Hall Masons;
  - Past Grand Treasurer, MWPHGL of Illinois;
  - Past Right Eminent Grand Commander and Past Grand Treasurer, Prince Hall Grand Commandery, Knights Templar (Illinois);

- o Suspended John G. Jones indefinitely in 1903 and expelled him from Freemasonry in 1904
- **Fields, Milton**
  - o *see Key Illinoisans of the Fields Faction*
- **Graham, Henry** (Chicago, Illinois)
  - o Charter Commander-In-Chief of Excelsior Consistory (USSC);
  - o Charter Commander-In-Chief, Occidental Consistory (SC-NWJ);
  - o Past Right Eminent Grand Commander, Prince Hall Grand Commandery of Knights Templar (Illinois);
  - o Charter Imperial Treasurer, AAONMS (Fields Faction)
- **Harris, Benjamin S.** (Chicago, Illinois)
  - o Past Commander-In-Chief, Occidental Consistory (SC-NWJ);
  - o Past Right Eminent Grand Commander, Prince Hall Grand Commandery of Knights Templar (Illinois);

- o Charter Imperial Potentate, AAONMS (Fields Faction)
- **Moore, Joseph W.** (Chicago, Illinois)
  - o Elder brother of Richard E. Moore;
  - o Past Master of North Star Lodge #1;
  - o Past Grand Master of Illinois Prince Hall Masons;
  - o Charter Most Excellent Grand High Priest of Holy Royal Arch Masons (Illinois);
  - o Past Eminent Commander, Godfrey Commandery #5;
  - o Past Right Eminent Grand Commander, Prince Hall Grand Commandery of Knights Templar (Illinois);
  - o Charter Potentate, Arabic Temple, AAONMS (Chicago, Illinois); Charter member of Excelsior Consistory (USSC);
  - o Charter member of Occidental Consistory (SC-NWJ);

- - Suspended John G. Jones and Theodore Wellington Jones in 1887 from the Grand Lodge and later reinstated them;
  - 1st black South Town Clerk
- **Moore, Richard E.** (Chicago, Illinois)
  - Past Master and charter Junior Warden of Hiram Lodge #14;
  - Past Senior Grand Warden and Past Grand Secretary, MWPHGL of Illinois;
  - Past Excellent High Priest, St. Mark's Chapter #1, HRAM;
  - Past Grand Secretary, Most Excellent Prince Hall Grand Chapter, Holy Royal Arch Masons (Illinois);
  - Past Eminent Commander, St. George Commandery #4;
  - Past Right Eminent Grand Commander and Past Grand Recorder, Prince Hall Grand Commandery of Knights Templar (Illinois);
  - Charter Recorder, Arabic Temple AAONMS (Chicago, Illinois);

- o Past Imperial Recorder, AAONMS (Fields Faction); Charter Recorder of Excelsior Consistory (USSC);
- o Charter Grand Secretary of Occidental Consistory (SC-NWJ); Past Grand Minister of State and Past Secretary General (SC-NWJ);
- o Past Lieutenant Grand Commander and Past Deputy for the Orient of Illinois (USC-NJ)
- **Smith, George J.** (Chicago, Illinois)
  - o Past Master of John Jones Lodge #7;
  - o Past Most Excellent Grand High Priest of Holy Royal Arch Masons (Illinois);
  - o Charter Right Eminent Grand Commander, Prince Hall Grand Commander of Knights Templar (Illinois)
- **Taylor, James W.** (Chicago, Illinois)
  - o Charter Worshipful Master of Hiram Lodge #14;
  - o Past Grand Master of Illinois Prince Hall Masons;

- o Past Most Excellent Grand High Priest, Most Excellent Prince Hall Grand Chapter, Holy Royal Arch Masons (Illinois);
- o Charter member of Excelsior Consistory (USSC);
- o Charter member of Occidental Consistory (SC-NWJ)

Key Illinoisans of the Fields Faction

The Fields Faction refers to the primary supporters of Milton Fields at the national levels in the Scottish Rite and Shrine organizations. Fields was a supporter of the Moore faction as who reciprocated in his efforts to expand the SC-NWJ and AAONMS (Fields Faction).

- **Dickerson, Dr. Egbert S.** (Cairo, Illinois)
    - Past Master of Lincoln Lodge #5;
    - Past Right Eminent Grand Commander and Past Grand Recorder, Prince Hall Grand Commandery of Knights Templar (Illinois);
    - Member, SC-NWJ;

- - 1st Deputy for the Orient of Illinois (USC-NJ);
  - Member, AAONMS (Fields Faction)
- **Fields, Milton** (St. Louis, Missouri)
  - Sovereign Grand Commander, SC-NWJ;
  - Past Deputy of Missouri (USC-NJ & USC-SJ);
  - Past Imperial Potentate, AAONMS;
  - Past Imperial Potentate, AEAONMS;
  - Charter Most Excellent Grand High Priest of Holy Royal Arch Masons (Missouri);
  - Past Right Eminent Grand Commander (Missouri);
  - Founder, Heroines of the Templar Crusades;
  - Charter Imperial Recorder, AAONMS
- **Harris, Benjamin S.**
  - *see Key Members of Moore Faction*
- **Moore, Joseph W.**
  - *see Key Members of Moore Faction*
- **Moore, Richard E.**
  - *see Key Members of Moore Faction*
- **Taylor, James W.**
  - *see Key Members of Moore Faction*

Appendix E:
AFRO-AMERICAN MEDIA

The primary forms of media utilized to communicate activities and leadership of Afro-American fraternal organizations were the newspapers and directories. While Black Newspapers covered the entire diaspora of activities, mainstream newspapers also covered some facet of their activities. In both instances, there was no distinguishing between legitimate and bogus bodies unless their status was called out in the articles themselves.

Directories also captured the names of the organizations and their leaders, in many instances, during the 19th and 20th Centuries. When corroborating the publication with Proceedings from fraternal organizations, one can verify the accuracy. In few instances, names were published in the directories after sessions for the state-wide bodies occurred. With this in mind, there are instances where names of elected officials may have been one year behind due to the timelines of publication.

With the technological advents of the late 20th and early 21st Centuries, digital versions of newspapers and directories are available online. Colleges and Universities have digital collections that are available to the public. The Library of Congress archives are available for digital searches of articles, directories, photographs and illustrations. The archive in Newspapers.com is very extensive as well as other resources aligned with Ancestry.com. While some may cost a fee, most of these resources are free. Those items in the public domain can be utilized for private works.

Newspapers referenced via Newspapers.com and the Library of Congress:

- The Altamont News (Illinois)
- The Appeal (Minnesota)
  - Western Appeal
- Asheville Citizen-Times (Illinois)
- The Birmingham News (Alabama)
- The Broad Ax (Utah)
- The Buffalo Sunday Morning News (New York)
- The Bystander (Iowa)
- Chicago Tribune (Illinois)
  - Chicago Daily Tribune
- Chicago Daily Telegraph (Illinois)

- The Daily Democrat (Iowa)
- The Dispatch (Missouri)
- The Enterprise (Massachusetts)
- Evening Star (District of Columbia)
- Herald News (Illinois)
- Indianapolis Recorder (Indiana)
- The Inter Ocean (Illinois)
- The Kansas City Times (Missouri)
- The Montana Plaindealer (Montana)
- The Montgomery Advisor (Alabama)
- Nashville Journal (Illinois)
- Natchez Democrat (Mississippi)
- Richmond Planet (Virginia)
- The Rock Island Argus (Illinois)
- St. Louis Globe-Democrat (Missouri)
- The Statesman (Louisiana)
- The Topeka Plaindealer (Kansas)
- The Topeka State Journal (Kansas)
- The Washington Bee (District of Columbia)
- The Wilkes Barre Weekly Times (Pennsylvania)

Directories referenced:

- Colored Peoples Blue Book and Business Directory – Chicago, Illinois
- The Lakeside City Directory – Chicago Illinois

Glossary of Terms

Accepted: Ritualistic customs and modes of operation that are accepted as legitimate practices in Freemasonry.

Allied Masonic Degrees: Refers to a series of Degrees:

- Ark Mariner
- Secret Monitor
- Knights of Constantine
- Knights of Three Kings
- Knights of Christian Mark
- Knights of the Holy Sepulchre
- Holy and Illustrious Cross

Ancient: Traditions are in alignment with the ancient usages and are accepted as a legitimate lineage in Freemasonry.

Ancient & Accepted: Ritualistic customs, modes of operation and traditions that are in alignment with ancient usages that align with a legitimate lineage and are accepted as legitimate practices in Freemasonry.

Ancient & Accepted Scottish Rite of Freemasonry (AASR):
See Ancient & Accepted; See Scottish Rite.

Blue Department/Blue House/Blue Lodge: Refers to a Masonic Lodge or Symbolic Lodge Degrees.

Bogus: Term used to describe organizations without a legitimate lineage.

Chapter:

- York Rite - A congregation of Holy Royal Arch Masons organized under the Constitution and Bylaws of a Grand Chapter of Holy Royal Arch Masons;
- Scottish Rite – A congregation of Fraters of a Chapter of the House of the Rose Croix (see Scottish Rite);
- Eastern Star – A congregation of members of the Order of the Eastern Star.

Clandestine: See Bogus.

Commander-In-Chief (CIC): Presiding officer of a Consistory.

Commandery: York Rite - A congregation of Knights Templar organized under the Constitution and Bylaws of a Grand Commandery of Knights Templar.

Consistory: A local body of the Scottish Rite and the Series of Degrees in the Scottish Rite System covering the 19th through the 32nd Degrees.

Council: York Rite - A congregation of Royal and Select Masters organized under the Constitution and Bylaws of a Grand Council of Royal and Select Masters.

Craft: See Freemason.

Crown: Ceremonial cap worn by Scottish Rite Masons. The act of crowning refers to the inculcation of a Scottish Rite Mason with the 33rd Degree.

Deputy or Deputy Inspector General: An appointed officer of a Supreme Council who oversees an Orient. He is the presiding officer of a Council of Deliberation or the Most Illustrious Commander-In-Chief for the Orient.

Elevation: The process of inculcating a Master Mason with the 4th through the 32nd Degrees. See Sublime Prince.

Fez: Ceremonial headgear worn by Shriners.

Frater: A Scottish Rite Mason.

Freemason: A member of a Lodge of Freemasons.

- An Entered Apprentice Mason has only been invested with the 1st Degree of Freemasonry.
- A Fellow Craft Mason has been invested with the 2nd Degree of Freemasonry.
- A Master Mason has been invested with the 3rd Degree of Freemasonry.

Freemasonry: A fraternal organization that provides a series of three Masonic Degrees on men who are of a specified age and believe in a Supreme Being.

Grand East: Headquarters of a Grand Lodge.

Grand Inspector General (GIG): An honorary member of a Supreme Council who has been crowned a 33rd Mason.

Grand Lodge: A Masonic jurisdiction consisting of Lodges.

Grand Master: Presiding officer of a Grand Lodge.

Grand Minister of State: The third ranking officer of a Supreme Council.

Holy Empire: The jurisdiction of a Supreme Council.

House: A distinct body within Freemasonry.

Illustrious: A salutation for Scottish Rite Masons who have been elevated to the 33rd Degree or have been elected to the Office of Commander-In-Chief of a Consistory.

Junior Warden (JW): Third in command of a Lodge.

Jurisdiction: A geographical designation, like a state or a region, over which a Masonic House maintains control.

Lieutenant Grand Commander: The second ranking officer of a Supreme Council.

Lodge: A congregation of Freemasons organized under the Constitution and Bylaws of a Grand Lodge.

Mason: See Freemason.

Masonic: Of or about Freemasonry.

Masonry: See Freemasonry.

Noble: Member of a Temple of Shriners.

Orient: A designated geographical area within a jurisdiction under the control of a Supreme Council.

Past Master (PM): A former Worshipful Master.

Potentate: The presiding officer of a Temple of Shriners.

Prince Hall Affiliation or Prince Hall Affiliated (PHA): Refers to bodies that can trace their roots to the charter of African Lodge #459, the original Lodge chartered by Prince Hall.

Priory: York Rite - A congregation of Knights of the York Cross of Honor organized under the Constitution and Bylaws of a Grand Priory.

Puissant: "Powerful"

Rite: A system of ceremonial and ritualistic practices.

Scottish Rite: Refers to a series of Masonic Degrees conferred upon Master Masons from the 4th to the 32nd. Select Sublime Princes are crowned Grand Inspectors General and receive the 33rd and last Degree. The Scottish Rite, considered the University of Freemasonry, operates under one central authority although degrees are organized under specific Scottish Rite Houses:

- Lodge of Perfection
- Chapter of the Rose Croix
- The Consistory.

Senior Warden (SW): Second in command of Lodge.

Shrine: Refers to the Ancient Egyptian Arabic Order Nobles of the Mystic Shrine fraternal organization.

Shriner: A member of the Shrine organization.

Sovereign Grand Commander: A Sovereign Grand Inspector General who is the presiding officer of a Supreme Council.

Sovereign Grand Inspector General (SGIG): A Grand Inspector General who has been elevated from honorary to actual membership in a Supreme Council. Active members have full voting privileges while Emeriti have limited voting privileges. Past Actives also have limited voting privileges.

Spurious: See Bogus.

Sublime Prince (SP): A Mason who has been elevated to the 32nd Degree.

Supreme Council (SC): Governing body of the Scottish Rite.

Temple:

- Blue House - A Masonic Lodge Hall;
- Shriners - A congregation of Shriners organized under the Constitution and Bylaws of the Ancient Egyptian Arabic Order Nobles of the Mystic Shrine.

Under Dispensation (UD or U.D.): Refers to an unchartered Lodge that was organized under a dispensation granted by a Grand Master on behalf of a Grand Lodge.

Worshipful Master: Elected leader of a Masonic Lodge.

York Rite: Refers to a series of progressive Masonic Degrees organized into separate York Rite Houses operating under its own authority:

- Holy Royal Arch Masons (HRAM)
- Royal and Select Masters (RSM)
- Knights Templar (KT)

- Knights of the York Cross of Honor (KYCH):
  - Honorary York Rite House designated for leaders who have presided over a:
    - Chapter of Holy Royal Arch Masons;
    - Council of Royal and Select Masters;
    - Commandery of Knights Templar.

About the Author

Daryl Lamar Andrews is a celebrated Masonic author and historian who has published multiple works on Masonic history and faith. With over twenty-five years of Freemasonry under his belt and several books in circulation, his expertise has been tried and tested resulting in his works being recognized across the world.

Other works by Daryl Lamar Andrews:

- *Masonic Abolitionists: Freemasonry and the Underground Railroad in Illinois*
- *Personification of Hope: A Legacy of National African American Political Leadership*
- *Valiance: Dynamics of True Faith and Brotherhood in a Changing World*

www.ingramcontent.com/pod-product-compliance
Lightning Source LLC
Chambersburg PA
CBHW061735270326
41928CB00011B/2238